Praise for *The Truth about Hell*

"Dan Burke and Patrick O'Hearn, in their book *The Truth about Hell*, address a growing concern in Christianity today: the denial of Hell. As more Christians dismiss this fundamental doctrine, Burke and O'Hearn remind us of St. Paul's exhortation to 'work out your own salvation with fear and trembling' (Phil. 2:12). To deny Hell is to deny love itself, for we cannot grasp the depth of God's love without acknowledging what He sacrificed to save us. Jesus, through His own words, warned of Hell's reality; this book powerfully reaffirms this truth, helping readers fully appreciate the lengths to which God goes to bring us into His love."

—Simone Rizkallah, Director, Philos Catholic

"In today's world, Hell is either ignored or sensationalized. One either doesn't need to worry about it or is completely consumed with images of eternal fires and endless tortures. In *The Truth about Hell*, however, Dan Burke and Patrick O'Hearn cut through this false dichotomy to give the actual truth about this important topic. By focusing on the teachings of Christ, His Church, and the saints, Burke and O'Hearn lay out what every Christian should know about Hell and what we can and should do to avoid it."

—Eric Sammons, Editor in Chief, *Crisis Magazine*

"The Lord Jesus commanded us to 'fear him who … has power to cast into hell' (Luke 12:5). Yet He also said, 'The truth will make you free' (John 8:32). Dan Burke and Patrick O'Hearn have produced an important text that is faithful to Jesus Christ and His insistence on the liberating truth about Hell. No one wants to talk about Hell, but, as the saints have declared, anyone who considers the reality of eternal punishment is truly set free from

all earthly cares and is galvanized in prayer and spiritual warfare. As such, this book will help many pious souls as well as many souls for whom the truth about Hell has been obscured."
—Timothy S. Flanders, Author, *City of God vs. City of Man*

"Dan Burke and Patrick O'Hearn offer Catholics a complete understanding of the Church's teaching on Hell. St. John of the Cross wrote, 'In the twilight of life, we shall be judged on love.' May this book move souls to the heights of God's love."
—Robert Nugent, Irish Catholic Vlogger and Commentator

The Truth about Hell

Also by Dan Burke
from Sophia Institute Press

Finding Peace in the Storm

Spiritual Warfare and the Discernment of Spirits

The Devil in the Castle

Into the Deep

Also by Patrick O'Hearn
from Sophia Institute Press

Our Lady of Sorrows

Nursery of Heaven (co-author)

Dan Burke and Patrick O'Hearn

The Truth about Hell

Through the Wisdom of Jesus, Mary, and the Magisterium

SOPHIA INSTITUTE PRESS

Manchester, New Hampshire

Sophia Institute Press
Box 5284, Manchester, NH 03108
1-800-888-9344
www.SophiaInstitute.com

Sophia Institute Press® is a registered trademark of Sophia Institute.

paperback ISBN 979-8-88911-354-6
ebook ISBN 979-8-88911-355-3

Library of Congress Control Number: 2024949056

First printing

*This work is dedicated to all those priests
who have heard our confessions through the years.*

If eternity were a doubtful matter, we ought even then to
make every effort in our power to escape an eternity of
torments; but no, it is not a matter of doubt; it is a truth
of faith, that after this life each of us must go into eternity,
to be forever in glory, or forever in despair.

—St. Alphonsus Liguori

Contents

Appendices

The Truth about Hell

Introduction

In his First Letter to the Corinthians, St. Paul penned one of the most beautiful lines in Sacred Scripture concerning Heaven: "What no eye has seen, nor ear heard, nor the heart of man conceived, what God has prepared for those who love him" (2:9). No person can fathom the sheer joy and blessedness that await him in Heaven. Gazing upon the Beatific Vision forever is the ultimate desire of the human heart, and it is also God's desire for every soul. One million years from now, those in Heaven will still be enraptured in wonder and awe at the most glorious sight, and it will feel like only a beginning. It is more intuitive, and certainly more consoling, to ponder Heaven than Hell. Heaven puts our souls at ease. It's the reason there are more books and movies on Heaven than on Hell.

What if St. Paul said the following: "What no eye has seen, nor ear heard, nor the heart of man conceived, what God has prepared for those who do *not* love Him"? God forces no man to receive the gift of Heaven. He sends no one to Hell; man sends himself there. The thought of Hell is among the most disturbing of considerations, or at least it should be. Imagine the worst pain, the hottest fire, the most rancid smell, and the most horrifying thing on earth, and multiply that by infinity, and you still have not touched the reality of Hell's torments. No one can fully conceive what Hell is like, though Jesus and the saints mentioned in this book will give you a glimpse of what awaits those who reject God and how we all can avoid that most horrifying end.

The Catholic Church does not preach and teach about Hell to scare people into coming to Mass, though the fear of Hell often leads souls to imperfect contrition.[1] The experience of Hell is the result of mankind's free will, not God's malice. French novelist Léon Bloy said in *La femme pauvre*, "The only real sadness, the only real failure, the only great tragedy in life, is not to become a saint." And since only saints are in Heaven, the greatest tragedy is to go to Hell. Of course, Purgatory is a temporary consequence of sin for the soul who dies in a state of grace. Sin involves choosing mere seconds of pleasure with the possibility of forfeiting a life of eternal happiness.

Where does the term *Hell* come from? It has its origins in Old English and Germanic languages. In Old English, the word was *hel*, describing the underworld or a place of the dead. Since the New Testament was primarily written in Greek, the notion of Hell often refers to *Gehenna*, a valley outside Jerusalem associated with fire and destruction, and *Hades*, the realm of the dead.

Jesus made it clear that Hell is real and permanent. He did not shy away from preaching on Hell, though many of His "followers" have—especially in our time. Of course, among the most desired deceptions of the devil is to make you believe that he does not exist and that Hell is not real.

In this work, we will explore what Jesus said about Hell, and we will reflect on Scripture passages pertaining to Hell as well as what the Church teaches, what the Doctors of the Church say, what the saints saw, and what Marian apparitions reveal about

---

[1] *Imperfect contrition* refers to sorrow for one's sins because of fear of the punishment of Hell.

Hell. Jesus has prepared a place in His Father's house for His true sons and daughters, but He forces no one to come. Instead, many have and will continue to choose Satan's horror house, a place of never-ending torture, pain, and remorse—a place that could be our final destination if we do not repent and embrace the love and redemption of God.

1

What Jesus Said about Hell

Jesus Christ, the second Person of the Blessed Trinity, the One who overturned the tables in the Temple and drove out the money changers, who called out the Pharisees and the scribes for their hypocrisy, does not mince words when it comes to sin and to our eternal fate. Our King wears a crown of thorns to show us that "the wages of sin is death" (Rom. 6:23)—eternal death. And Christ the King will return to separate the sheep from the goats. The goats, the unrighteous, "will go away into eternal punishment" and the sheep, the righteous, "into eternal life" (Matt. 25:46).

Throughout Scripture, Jesus is direct, clear, and stern when it comes to Hell. This sternness is not what we see in the grumpy old guy who shouts threats at kids for running on his lawn. It is more akin to the mother who cries out with full voice at her small child as he is about to wander into traffic. Jesus' motivation is rooted in a deep love and desire for all to know salvation. He came with compassion and mercy—not "to call the righteous, but sinners to repentance" (Luke 5:32). He began His public ministry with these words: "The time is fulfilled, and the kingdom of God is at hand; repent, and believe in the gospel" (Mark 1:15). Repentance and Hell go together: if there were no Hell, there would be no need for repentance. Jesus deeply desires that everyone be saved (see 1 Tim. 2:4), but many do not want to be saved. They would rather "save" themselves (which is not possible) than be saved by Him whose blood was poured out for their forgiveness and salvation.

Jesus directly references Hell numerous times in the Gospels. St. Matthew's Gospel includes nine references, and St. Mark, St. Luke, and St. John have one reference each as seen in the following verses. While there are many important passages that also deal with Hell from the standpoint of the result of the Final Judgment, these passages deal directly with the reality and nature of Hell:

> But I say to you that every one who is angry with his brother shall be liable to judgment; whoever insults his brother shall be liable to the council, and whoever says, "You fool!" shall be liable to the hell of fire. (Matt. 5:22)

> Every tree that does not bear good fruit is cut down and thrown into the fire. (Matt. 7:19)

> I tell you, many will come from east and west and sit at table with Abraham, Isaac, and Jacob in the kingdom of heaven, while the sons of the kingdom will be thrown into the outer darkness; there men will weep and gnash their teeth. (Matt. 8:11–12)

> And do not fear those who kill the body but cannot kill the soul; rather fear him who can destroy both soul and body in hell. (Matt. 10:28).

> The Son of man will send his angels, and they will gather out of his kingdom all causes of sin and all evildoers, and throw them into the furnace of fire; there men will weep and gnash their teeth. (Matt. 13:41–42)

Woe to the world for temptations to sin! For it is necessary that temptations come, but woe to the man by whom the temptation comes! And if your hand or your foot causes you to sin, cut it off and throw it from you; it is better for you to enter life maimed or lame than with two hands or two feet to be thrown into the eternal fire. And if your eye causes you to sin, pluck it out and throw it from you; it is better for you to enter life with one eye than with two eyes to be thrown into the hell of fire. (Matt. 18:7–9)

But when the king came in to look at the guests, he saw there a man who had no wedding garment; and he said to him, "Friend, how did you get in here without a wedding garment?" And he was speechless. Then the king said to the attendants, "Bind him hand and foot, and cast him into the outer darkness; there men will weep and gnash their teeth." For many are called, but few are chosen. (Matt. 22:11–14)

And cast the worthless servant into the outer darkness; there men will weep and gnash their teeth. (Matt. 25:30)

Then he will say to those at his left hand, "Depart from me, you cursed, into the eternal fire prepared for the devil and his angels." (Matt. 25:41)

Whoever causes one of these little ones who believe in me to sin, it would be better for him if a great millstone were hung round his neck and he were thrown into the sea. And if your hand causes you to sin, cut it off; it is better for you to enter life maimed than with two hands to go to hell, to the unquenchable fire. And if your foot causes you to sin, cut it off; it is better for you to enter life lame than with two feet to be thrown into hell. And if your eye causes you to sin, pluck it out; it is better for you to enter the kingdom of God with one eye than with two eyes to be thrown into hell. (Mark 9:42–47)

The poor man died and was carried by the angels to Abraham's bosom. The rich man also died and was buried; and in Hades, being in torment, he lifted up his eyes, and saw Abraham far off and Lazarus in his bosom. And he called out, "Father Abraham, have mercy upon me, and send Lazarus to dip the end of his finger in water and cool my tongue; for I am in anguish in this flame." (Luke 16:22–24)

I am the vine, you are the branches. He who abides in me, and I in him, he it is that bears much fruit, for apart from me you can do nothing. If a man does not abide in me, he is cast forth as a branch and withers; and the branches are gathered, thrown into the fire and burned. (John 15:5–6)

Reflect on the word Jesus uses in these twelve Scripture passages: *fire* (used eight times), *gnash their teeth*, *weep*, *darkness*, *flame*, and *burn*. These words are far from comforting; they are deeply troubling. Jesus' blunt words are also the opposite of how Heaven is described by St. John in the book of Revelation: "He will wipe away every tear from their eyes, and death shall be no more, neither shall there be mourning nor crying nor pain any more, for the former things have passed away" (21:4).

The *Gehenna that Jesus speaks about* was a valley southwest of Jerusalem. In this dark, ominous valley, children were burned in sacrifice to the pagan god Moloch. Consequently, the Jews referred to Gehenna as "the abode of the damned," a term later adopted by Jesus.[2] So when Jesus used the word *Gehenna*, the Jews knew exactly what He was referring to: Hell itself. Furthermore, the term *Gehenna* is used twelve times in the New Testament, eleven times by Jesus.[3] Sadly, many continue to distort Jesus' teaching and ignore these clear references to Hell. Satan tempted Eve with these words: "Did God say, 'You shall not eat of any tree of the garden?'" (Gen. 3:1); and he likewise continues to plant doubt in man's mind: "Did Jesus really say Hell exists? Was He not speaking figuratively? Surely, an all-loving God would never send anyone to Hell!" "Surely we can hope that all will be saved and that Hell is just a psychological manipulation."

Satan wants us not only to doubt Jesus' words, especially about Hell, but even to distort them. Thus, many focus exclusively on Heaven while others imagine a world without consequences. "Just don't kill anyone" or "Just be a good person" are the words that many parishioners and children hear from their "spiritual fathers" and "parents" even when they are playing with fire—that is, living in mortal sin. Priests who remain silent on contraception and parents who condone their children's fornication will also be held accountable for such sins.

At the same time, we ought not to live simply to avoid Hell. No one who lives with this as his primary motive lives in the joy, peace, and freedom Jesus promises to those who follow Him to Heaven. The authentic disciple of Jesus lives entirely for God and for Heaven. We want to be worthy of the wedding banquet of Heaven, which is possible only by God's grace.

---

[2] Joseph Hontheim, "Hell," *The Catholic Encyclopedia*, vol. 7 (New York: Robert Appleton, 1910), https://www.newadvent.org/cathen/07207a.htm.

[3] Tim Staples, "What Is Hell?," *Catholic Answers*, November 8, 2021, https://www.catholic.com/magazine/online-edition/what-is-Hell.

In the parable of the wedding banquet found in the Gospels of Sts. Matthew and Luke, Jesus likens the Kingdom of Heaven to a king who prepared a marriage feast for his son. The king's servants call those who were invited to attend, but many rejected the invitation. Many were "not worthy" to attend (Matt. 22:8). So the king commanded his servants to invite as many people as possible, both the good and the bad. And when the banquet hall was full, the king came to check out the guests. Noticing one guest without a wedding garment, the king declared, "Friend, how did you get in here without a wedding garment?' And he was speechless. Then the king said to the attendants, 'Bind him hand and foot, and cast him into the outer darkness; there men will weep and gnash their teeth.' For many are called, but few are chosen" (Matt. 22:11–14). According to *The Navarre Bible*, "the wedding garment represents the dispositions necessary for admission to the kingdom."[4] Specifically, St. Augustine stated that love is the wedding garment—a love that arises "from a pure heart and a good conscience and sincere faith" (1 Tim. 1:5).[5]

Several Doctors of the Church have interpreted this passage and Matthew 7:14[6] as evidence that more people will be damned than saved. The consensus of opinion among the writers in the early Church and into the Middle Ages was that only a minority of persons will be saved. The Church, however, does not make any definitive statement about the number of people who will be saved.

---

[4] *The Navarre Bible: St Matthew's Gospel* (New York: Scepter Publishers, 2005), 208.

[5] Quoted in "Commentary on the Gospel: The Wedding Garment," Opus Dei, https://opusdei.org/en-ph/gospel/commentary-on-the-gospel-the-wedding-garment/#_ftn3.

[6] "For the gate is narrow and the way is hard, that leads to life, and those who find it are few."

For instance, St. John of the Cross wrote, "Reflect that many are called but few chosen and that, if you are not careful, your perdition is more certain than your salvation, especially since the path to eternal life is so narrow."[7] St. Alphonsus Liguori added, "The way to Heaven is straight and narrow: they who wish to arrive at that place of bliss by walking in the paths of pleasure shall be disappointed; and therefore few reach it, because few are willing to use violence to themselves in resisting temptations."[8] The violence St. Alphonsus talks about is the spiritual discipline of fasting, prayer, and avoiding the near occasions of sin. St. Teresa of Avila would frequently tell preachers: "Preach, O my priests, preach against bad confessions; for it is on account of bad confessions that the greater part of Christians are damned."[9]

Make no mistake: Jesus invites and desires everyone to the wedding banquet of Heaven. In fact, His love and desire run so deep that He openly wept over Jerusalem because so many refused His love and salvation (Matt. 23:37–39). He wills that no one be lost. "And this is the will of him who sent me, that I should lose nothing of all that he has given me, but raise it up at the last day" (John 6:39). Sadly, many do not even bother to RSVP to the gift of eternal life. They prefer another venue with a different master—Satan the destroyer, the torturer, the slave master. And if they do show up, they likely have not prepared for the sublimity of the feast. Barring the Satanists, however, most people do not

---

7   *The Collected Works of St. John of the Cross*, trans. Kieran Kavanaugh, O.C.D., and Otilio Rodriguez, O.C.D. (Washington, D.C.: ICS Publications, 1973), 673.

8   *The Sermons of St. Alphonsus Liguori*, 51.

9   Quoted in St. Alphonsus Liguori, *Preaching* (New York: Benziger Brothers, 1890), 546.

want to spend eternity in Hell; they just don't believe that such a place exists, or they believe they don't deserve to go there.

Keep in mind: Hell is not just for the most wretched of humanity. Many who would consider themselves "good" will, according to Jesus' warnings, end up in Hell. In the book of Revelation, Jesus offers a stern admonition for the lukewarm: "I know your works: you are neither cold nor hot. Would that you were cold or hot! So, because you are lukewarm, and neither cold nor hot, I will spew you out of my mouth" (Revelation 3:15–16). We, too, can forfeit Heaven not only for being lukewarm but also for other sins, such as anger. As Jesus reminds us, "But I say to you that every one who is angry with his brother shall be liable to judgment; whoever insults his brother shall be liable to the council, and whoever says, 'You fool!' shall be liable to the hell of fire" (Matt. 5:22).

Still, St. Dismas gives us hope in God's mercy, provided that we repent. St. Dismas, one of the criminals crucified next to Jesus on the Cross, said, "Jesus, remember me when you come in your kingly power." And Jesus replied, "Truly, I say to you, today you will be with me in Paradise" (Luke 23:42–43). Thus, the "good thief," St. Dismas, stole Paradise, while the bad thief (the other one crucified next to Jesus) did not appear to do so. The bad thief's heart was hardened.

In Luke 12:48, Jesus reminds us of our great responsibility as Christians: "Every one to whom much is given, of him will much be required; and of him to whom men commit much they will demand the more." To be a member of Christ's true Church, the Catholic Church, and to receive Jesus' Body, Blood, Soul, and Divinity in the Holy Eucharist is the greatest gift from God. Christ nourishes, sustains, and strengthens us with the Holy Eucharist. Hence, Jesus expects much of us. That is why He can say to each of us: "Every tree that does not bear good fruit is cut down and thrown into the fire" (Matt. 7:19). Our Lord gives us every grace we need to reach Heaven, but many reject that grace or treat it as if it were not important. The end result for both is the same.

Jesus tells us throughout Scripture not to be afraid. But on one occasion, He does tell us to fear something: "And do not fear those who kill the body but cannot kill the soul; rather fear him who can destroy both soul and body in hell" (Matt. 10:28). Jesus clearly teaches that we ought to fear losing Heaven. We ought to fear ending up in Hell, where our body and our soul will be tortured forever and, even more importantly, be forever separated from the vision of God.

Our most important earthly task is to reach Heaven and to bring as many people with us as possible, especially those under our care. If we fall short of that noble calling, we have lost everything, "for what does it profit a man, to gain the whole world and forfeit his life?" (Mark 8:36).

One of the clearest and most startling parables concerning Hell involves the rich man and Lazarus in St. Luke's Gospel (16:19–31). If we have any doubt that Hell is real or permanent, we need only to read this parable. "There was a rich man, who was clothed in purple and fine linen and who feasted sumptuously every day. And at his gate lay a poor man named Lazarus, full of sores, who desired to be fed with what fell from the rich man's table" (16:19–21). The rich man, whose name is not given,[10] goes to Hell after his death, while the poor man, Lazarus, goes to "Abraham's bosom," a place of rest. (This Lazarus is not to be confused with the Lazarus whom Jesus raised from the dead.) The rich man is in torment, while Lazarus is in peace. The rich man had lived a luxurious life, while the poor man had experienced the opposite. When the rich man

---

[10] He is sometimes called Dives, Latin for "rich man."

asked Abraham why he suffered, Abraham said, "Son, remember that you in your lifetime received your good things, and Lazarus in like manner evil things; but now he is comforted here, and you are in anguish. And besides all this, between us and you a great chasm has been fixed, in order that those who would pass from here to you may not be able, and none may cross from there to us" (Luke 16:25–26).

But it was not the rich man's wealth that sent him to Hell; rather, it was his lack of charity, especially toward the poor. The rich man had ignored Lazarus's pleading. As Jesus says in Matthew's Gospel, "Depart from me, you cursed, into the eternal fire prepared for the devil and his angels; for I was hungry and you gave me no food, I was thirsty and you gave me no drink" (25:41–42).

One line of the parable of the rich man and Lazarus is critical to understanding the doctrine of Hell: "A great chasm has been fixed" between that place of rest and Hell, Abraham tells the rich man, and "none may cross from there to us" (Luke 16:26). There is no get-out-of-Hell card. The book of Revelation also testifies to this reality: "Now war arose in heaven, Michael and his angels fighting against the dragon; and the dragon and his angels fought, but they were defeated and there was no longer any place for them in heaven" (12:7–8). Once the fallen angels were kicked out of Heaven, they were not welcomed back. Period.

Perhaps Jesus does not name the rich man so that each one of us can realize that without grace and the virtue of charity, we, too, can end up in Hell. As seen in this parable, the rich man received good things in this life, while Lazarus received evil things. Throughout our lives, we vacillate between consolation and desolation, prosperity and adversity. One day, we are the rich man, feasting, and the next day, we are Lazarus, reduced to utter poverty, begging on our knees. St. Alphonsus Ligouri reminds us that "the essence of perfection is to embrace the will of God in all things, prosperous or adverse. In prosperity, even sinners find it easy to unite themselves to the divine will; but it takes saints to unite themselves to God's will when things go wrong and are painful to self-love."[11] Embracing the will of God in good and bad circumstances is the road to Heaven; avoiding the will of God is the path to Hell.

Although not included in the twelve Gospel references above referring to Hell, Jesus makes it clear that our actions have consequences with respect to the journey to Hell or Heaven: "Enter by the narrow gate; for the gate is wide and the way is easy, that leads to destruction, and those who enter by it are many. For the gate is narrow and the way is hard, that leads to life, and those who find it are few" (Matt. 7:13–14). We are faced with two roads, as the famed Robert Frost said in his poem "The Road Not Taken." The road to Hell is easy and worn down by many who have trodden it before us. It is a road filled with pleasure and as little pain as possible. In fact, this road takes a detour around the Cross and the sacrifice of Jesus for our sins.

On the other hand, Jesus reveals that the road to Heaven is the road less taken. "Few" choose this narrow road because it is "hard." It is filled with all types of suffering: betrayal, interior desolation, misunderstandings, physical pain, and persecution. This road goes straight to Calvary, where those who travel it come face-to-face with Jesus and join their sufferings with His for the sake of their salvation and that of the world. Those who take this road, even though it is less traveled, walk in the footsteps of Jesus and all the

---

[11] Quoted in Dan Burke, *Finding Peace in the Storm: Reflections on St. Alphonsus Liguori's* Uniformity with God's Will (Manchester, NH: Sophia Institute Press, 2023), 26.

saints before them. This is the trail of blood, sweat, and tears that leads to Heaven. It is the path of the red and white martyrs. And there is no other path to Heaven for Catholics. Each of us must decide which way we will follow: the way of the Cross or the way of the world. One path leads to eternal life while the other path leads to eternal destruction. One path was paved by Jesus; the other path was paved by Satan.

Let us return to the parable of the rich man and Lazarus. In the preceding chapter in St. Luke's Gospel is probably the most famous parable in Scripture: the parable of the prodigal son. This parable reveals the mercy and love of God, whereas the parable of the rich man and Lazarus reveals the justice of God. Hence, the mercy of God, particularly in the New Testament, tends to overshadow the justice of God. And yet Jesus, the face of the Heavenly Father, references Hell twelve times in the Gospels because He loves us so much, because He created us for unending communion with the Blessed Trinity. And as a result, He offered His life for the salvation of every soul, so that we might choose Him. "But God shows his love for us in that while we were yet sinners Christ died for us" (Rom. 5:8). How do we return such prodigious love?

Sadly, you will likely never see a Catholic church with a painting of the rich man and Lazarus, especially with the former surrounded in flames. You will, however, find images of the father embracing the prodigal son. Justice and mercy are not opposites; they are complementary. As St. Thomas Aquinas declared: "Justice and mercy are so united, that the one ought to be mingled with the other; justice without mercy is cruelty; mercy without justice, profusion—hence He goes on to the one from the other."[12]

---

[12] Thomas Aquinas, *Catena Aurea*, vol. 1, trans. William Whiston (London: J. G. F. and J. Rivington, 1842), 113.

One of Jesus' most striking messages concerning sin and Hell can be found in St. Mark's Gospel (9:42–47). Here Jesus reveals that it would be better for us to be thrown into the sea with millstones around our necks than to scandalize or somehow mislead others regarding the most important matters of faith. The passage of the millstone calls to mind Jesus' words at the Last Supper, when He describes Judas: "Woe to that man by whom the Son of man is betrayed! It would have been better for that man if he had not been born" (Matt. 26:24). Jesus, the Good Shepherd, provides a clear warning that we must live the Faith we claim and help others live it, or, by our rejection of this grace, we will live out an eternity in our chosen destination: Hell.

Jesus warns of "wolves in sheep's clothing." These wolves preach a different gospel from Jesus' (see Matt. 7:15). Their false gospel is devoid of authentic love because they fail to warn souls of the most horrifying end any soul will ever know. Without the bad news of Hell, the good news makes no sense. The Gospels are clear, and Jesus is clear: Hell is real. And the Gospels' clarity continues to build, as we will see in the next chapter.

Questions for Reflection

❖ What stood out, struck you, or
moved you in this chapter?

❖ Do you fear Hell? Why or why not?
What is this fear rooted in?

❖ Which of Jesus' teachings on Hell
speaks to you the most, and why?

❖ How can the reality of Hell help
or hinder your spiritual life?

❖ How does the contrasting mercy of God
strike you? How can we avail ourselves
more fully of this mercy and grace?

2

Other Scripture References to Hell

———◇———

Hell is not an afterthought, like some vague or subliminal message that is buried in Sacred Scripture for us to find and then debate whether it truly exists. Hell is one of the most prominent themes in the Gospels and throughout Sacred Scripture because Jesus came to save us from the fires of Hell by destroying sin and death. "The last enemy to be destroyed is death" (1 Cor. 15:26).

Sacred Scripture is inerrant—that is, without error. Hence, we cannot pick and choose which Scripture verses we accept or reject. The same is true of our Catholic Faith. If Jesus and the Catholic Church say that Hell is real, then it is real, because the Holy Spirit guided the authors of Scripture and still guides the Church to proclaim this truth. Quoting the Vatican II document *Dei Verbum*, the *Catechism of the Catholic Church* states: "Since therefore all that the inspired authors or sacred writers affirm should be regarded as affirmed by the Holy Spirit, we must acknowledge that the books of Scripture firmly, faithfully, and without error teach that truth which God, for the sake of our salvation, wished to see confided to the Sacred Scriptures" (CCC 107).

Even though Jesus' teachings on Hell in the Gospels are clear and comprehensive, the Holy Spirit inspired other writers of other books of the Bible to convey the reality of Hell. Following are

some prominent Old Testament and the New Testament references to Hell:

> And they shall go forth and look on the dead bodies of the
> men that have rebelled against me; for their worm shall not
> die, their fire shall not be quenched, and they shall be an
> abhorrence to all flesh. (Isa. 66:24).

> At that time shall arise Michael, the great prince who has
> charge of your people. And there shall be a time of trouble,
> such as never has been since there was a nation till that
> time; but at that time your people shall be delivered, every
> one whose name shall be found written in the book. And
> many of those who sleep in the dust of the earth shall
> awake, some to everlasting life, and some to shame and
> everlasting contempt. (Dan. 12:1–2)

> The soul that sins shall die. The son shall not suffer for the
> iniquity of the father, nor the father suffer for the iniquity
> of the son; the righteousness of the righteous shall be upon
> himself, and the wickedness of the wicked shall be upon
> himself. (Ezek. 18:20)

> The wicked shall depart to Sheol, all the nations that forget
> God. (Ps. 9:17)

> Let death come upon them; let them go down to Sheol
> alive; let them go away in terror into their graves. But I
> call upon God; and the Lord will save me. (Ps. 55:15–16)

> Sheol and Abaddon lie open before the Lord—how much
> more the hearts of men! (Prov. 15:11)

> The wise man's path leads upward to life, that he may avoid
> Sheol beneath. (Prov. 15:24)

If you beat him with the rod you will save his life from Sheol. (Prov. 23:14)

For thou wilt not abandon my soul to Hades, nor let thy Holy One see corruption. (Acts 2:27)

And the tongue is a fire. The tongue is an unrighteous world among our members, staining the whole body, setting on fire the cycle of nature, and set on fire by hell. (James 3:6)

God did not spare the angels when they sinned, but cast them into hell and committed them to pits of nether gloom to be kept until the judgment. (2 Pet. 2:4)

They shall suffer the punishment of eternal destruction and exclusion from the presence of the Lord and from the glory of his might. (2 Thess. 1:9)

And the angels that did not keep their own position but left their proper dwelling have been kept by him in eternal chains in the nether gloom until the judgment of the great day; just as Sodom and Gomorrah and the surrounding cities, which likewise acted immorally and indulged in un-natural lust, serve as an example by undergoing a punish-ment of eternal fire. (Jude 1:6–7)

And the smoke of their torment goes up for ever and ever; and they have no rest, day or night, these worshipers of the beast and its image, and whoever receives the mark of its name. (Rev. 14:11)

And the beast was captured, and with it the false prophet who in its presence had worked the signs by which he deceived those who had received the mark of the beast and those who worshiped its image. These two were thrown alive into the lake of fire that burns with brimstone. (Rev. 19:20)

And the sea gave up the dead in it, Death and Hades gave up the dead in them, and all were judged by what they had done. Then Death and Hades were thrown into the lake of fire. This is the second death, the lake of fire. (Rev. 20:13–14)

But as for the cowardly, the faithless, the polluted, as for murderers, fornicators, sorcerers, idolaters, and all liars, their lot shall be in the lake that burns with fire and brimstone, which is the second death. (Rev 21:8)

Long before Jesus became Incarnate, the Old Testament depicted Hell. This should not surprise us, since the New Testament is the fulfillment of the Old Testament. Indeed, Jesus was the greatest prophet of all, for He is God. All of the other prophets foreshadowed Jesus. The prophet Isaiah, who lived around the eighth century B.C., clearly warns about Hell. After all, the prophets tell us what we need to hear, not what we want to hear. Prophets beckon us to conversion. Isaiah prophesied mostly to the inhabitants of Judah, calling them to repent of their disobedience, or else judgment would be upon them. Specifically, Isaiah said: "And they shall go forth and look on the dead bodies of the men that have rebelled against me; for their worm shall not die, their fire shall not be quenched, and they shall be an abhorrence to all flesh" (66:24).

Since the Fall of Adam and Eve, mankind has rebelled against God. The word *rebellion* comes from the Latin *rebellionem*, meaning "rebellion, revolt; renewal of war."[13] Even before sin entered the world, a great war was incited by the ancient dragon and the fallen angels against St. Michael the Archangel and the good angels. Today the war rages on, as demons and man now rebel against God Himself. They rebel against truth, beauty, and goodness. God cannot reward sin; He can only forgive it. Thus, the unrepentant sinners' "fire shall not be quenched."

To better understand these Scripture references to Hell, it is worth noting that the translation of *Hell* can have various meanings. These include the Hebrew *Sheol* and the Greek *Hades*, *Tartarus*, and *Gehenna*.[14] *Sheol* describes the abode of the dead, where both the good and the bad go. *Sheol* means "the underworld, Hades."[15] As seen in the story of the rich man and Lazarus, a great chasm exists between the righteous and the unrighteous. The righteous live in peace, and the unrighteous in anguish. The New Testament frequently uses *Hades* instead of *Sheol*. *Hades* refers not to a place of punishment but to the realm of the dead. On the other hand, the term "Gehenna" consistently refers to a place of unending punishment for the wicked, according to Catholic teaching.[16]

Besides the prophet Isaiah, the prophet Daniel testifies to the certitude of Hell. Taken into captivity by King Nebuchadnezzar II during the Babylonian exile, around 605 B.C., Daniel interpreted dreams and offered prophetic visions. He describes the resurrection of the dead in these words:

---

13 *Online Etymology Dictionary*, s.v. "rebellion," updated May 16, 2021, https://www.etymonline.com/word/rebellion#etymonline _v_36896.

14 Staples, "What Is Hell?"

15 *Online Etymology Dictionary*, s.v. "Sheol," https://www.etymonline .com/search?q=sheol.

16 "Sheol."

At that time shall arise Michael, the great prince who has charge of your people. And there shall be a time of trouble, such as never has been since there was a nation till that time; but at that time your people shall be delivered, every one whose name shall be found written in the book. And many of those who sleep in the dust of the earth shall awake, some to everlasting life, and some to shame and everlasting contempt. (Dan. 12:1–2)

Daniel presents two destinations for man's final resting place: everlasting life and everlasting contempt. The term "everlasting" is key, describing something that is eternal or indefinite. Clearly, the notion of Heaven and Hell were present in the Old Testament, though not as defined as we know them today.

A few centuries before the prophet Daniel lived, King David, inspired by the Holy Spirit, wrote the Psalms. In two psalms, he speaks striking words about the afterlife. Psalm 9:17 says, "The wicked shall depart to Sheol, all the nations that forget God." So not only individuals, but nations will end up in Sheol. Judaism's understanding of Sheol developed over time from simply a place of the dead to a place for the righteous and the unrighteous. The righteous awaited the resurrection of the dead. After Jesus' Resurrection, however, Catholics saw Sheol in a new light. Sheol would now become Gehenna or Hell because Christ would bring the righteous out of the bosom of Abraham to Purgatory or Heaven while the wicked would remain.[17]

King David has another line that points to the real possibility of Sheol as place of pain: "Let death come upon them; let them go

[17] Fr. Charles Grondin, "Did Sheol Become Gehenna After the Resurrection?" Catholic Answers, https://www.catholic.com/qa /did-sheol-become-gehenna-after-the-resurrection.

down to Sheol alive; let them go away in terror into their graves. But I call upon God; and the Lord will save me" (Ps. 55:15–16). Sheol thus became associated with the notion of the grave or the pit, which creates fear and terror. The Psalms are filled with strong language and imagery and especially powerful prayers of protection against one's enemies. We would not desire Hell for anyone, even our worst enemy. The Psalms seek God's protection and justice against our foes, not revenge. As St. Paul reminds us, "Beloved, never avenge yourselves, but leave it to the wrath of God; for it is written, 'Vengeance is mine, I will repay, says the Lord'" (Rom. 12:19).

The Old Testament writers confront the stark reality of Hell, and the New Testament writers are even grimmer when it comes to Hell. "Eternal destruction," "eternal chains," "a lake of fire" are a few of the phrases that describe Hell. Such vivid and troubling descriptions of Hell seem like the worst nightmare. But the nightmare of Hell is no dream. It is real, and it never ends; the soul is eternal, and thus, its choice regarding Heaven or Hell is an eternal choice. There is no relief in Hell. And this nightmare can become a reality for us and all people if we fail to receive the gift of grace and forgiveness that Jesus offers us.

The last book of the Bible, the book of Revelation, or the Apocalypse, offers a glimpse into why Hell and Purgatory must exist. Written by St. John the Evangelist during his exile to the island of Patmos (present-day Greece), the book of Revelation issues a series of warnings. In regard to Heaven, it states: "But nothing unclean shall enter it, nor any one who practices abomination or falsehood, but only those who are written in the Lamb's book of life" (21:27). The purity of God, His utter holiness, prevents us from entering into His presence with the slightest blemish. Jesus Himself expresses this in the Beatitudes: "Blessed are the pure in heart, for they shall see God" (Matt. 5:8).

The inner sanctuary of the Jewish Temple, the Holy of Holies, was so sacred that only the high priest could enter it, once a year with some sacrifice for himself and the "errors of the people" (Heb. 9:7). It was the place of the *Shekhinah*, God's presence, and it housed the Ark of the Covenant, which contained the Ten Commandments, manna, and the rod of Aaron. It is no surprise, then, that Jesus drove out those who made His house a marketplace (see Matt. 21:12–13). If God's Temple on earth was treated with so much reverence, how much more the Temple of Heaven? None of us can enter Heaven on our own merits, no matter how holy we are. We need to be washed in Jesus' blood to reach Heaven, according to St. John: "Then one of the elders addressed me, saying, "Who are these, clothed in white robes, and whence have they come?" I said to him, "Sir, you know." And he said to me, "These are they who have come out of the great tribulation; they have washed their robes and made them white in the blood of the Lamb" (7:13–14).

In his First Letter to the Corinthians, St. Paul testifies to the purity of Heaven by revealing who will not be admitted. "Do you not know that the unrighteous will not inherit the kingdom of God? Do not be deceived; neither the immoral, nor idolaters, nor adulterers, nor homosexuals, nor thieves, nor the greedy, nor drunkards, nor revilers, nor robbers will inherit the kingdom of God" (6:9–10). If the unrighteous do not inherit Heaven, then where will they end up? Only one possibility exists according to St. Paul: Hell. As alluded to earlier, Jesus also said that the unrighteous, especially those who omit charitable works, "will go away into eternal punishment, but the righteous into eternal life" (Matt. 25:46). Yes, Hell is a real consequence not only of wicked deeds but also of failing to perform righteous works. Salvation is a pure gift from God that we cannot "earn"; we are saved by

God's grace. But we must cooperate with His grace by becoming authentic disciples of Jesus.[18]

Aside from Jesus' words, James 3:6 is the only other place we find the term *Gehenna* used, and it refers to "the fire of Gehenna" regarding the danger of an unruly tongue.[19] Not surprisingly, St. John Vianney described licentious talk as a "sewer" of Hell.[20] One who spews obscenities and blasphemous language imitates the demons, who curse God instead of blessing Him. An unruly tongue also leads to such sins as detraction, gossip, and slander. These sins violate the fifth commandment, "Thou shall not kill," because they literally destroy a person's good name. Slander and calumny also violate the eighth commandment by hurting another's reputation through lying. Detraction reveals a person's faults or shortcoming to others.

Many souls believe that such sins—if they even believe they *are* sins—could never send them to Hell. In his vision of the new Heaven and the new earth, where Jesus sat on His throne, St. John the Evangelist heard Jesus say the following: "But as for the cowardly, the faithless, the polluted, as for murderers, fornicators, sorcerers, idolaters, and all liars, their lot shall be in the lake that burns with fire and brimstone, which is the second death" (Rev. 21:8). Yes, Hell is not only populated with those who only committed grave sins, such as murder and fornication. No, lying, unbelief, cowardness, and sorcery (modern-day practices of the occult) can also send us for a *perpetual* swim in "the lake that burns with fire and brimstone."

---

[18] Learn more about what it means to be a disciple of Jesus in the "What Next?" section of this book.

[19] Staples, "What Is Hell?"

[20] "The Sewer of Hell," in *Sermons of the Curé of Ars — Excerpts*, Catholic Library Project, https://catholiclibrary.org/library/view?docId=/Tridentine-EN/XCT.086.html&chunk.id=00000037.

For those who doubt that Hell is permanent, the book of Revelation is clear:

> And another angel, a third, followed them, saying with a loud voice, "If any one worships the beast and its image, and receives a mark on his forehead or on his hand, he also shall drink the wine of God's wrath, poured unmixed into the cup of his anger, and he shall be tormented with fire and brimstone in the presence of the holy angels and in the presence of the Lamb. And the smoke of their torment goes up for ever and ever; and they have no rest, day or night, these worshipers of the beast and its image, and whoever receives the mark of its name." (14:9–11)

The torments in Hell never end for those who receive the mark of the beast. Because the devil cannot create anything but can only distort and mock what God does, the mark of the beast mocks the Sacrament of Baptism, in which we receive an indelible mark on our souls, configuring us to Christ and making us children of God.

To understand Hell better, we only need to look at Heaven. According to St. John, "And night shall be no more; they need no light of lamp or sun, for the Lord God will be their light, and they shall reign for ever and ever" (Rev. 22:5). In Heaven, God is all in all, the light that never fades; mercy, grace, and love never cease. In Hell, darkness envelops everything. The tormented soul turns inward on himself to a life of remorse and regret. Since Heaven is the perpetual adoration of God, filled with bliss, peace, and joy, Hell must be the opposite: perpetual disorientation filled with torment, pain, and misery.

But like Heaven, Hell will always remain a mystery, so the terms used by Jesus and the Scripture writers offer only a glimpse of eternity. But no analogy or parable can fully describe what Hell is truly like. Like a good father who warns his son about playing with fire, Jesus and the saints do not want us to get burned forever. And if Scripture isn't clear enough on the reality of Hell, Jesus founded the Catholic Church to make sure that there is no mistaking His teachings and there is a clear path to Heaven and God's love and mercy

Questions for Reflection

❖ What stood out, struck you, or
moved you in this chapter?

❖ Which Scripture passage on Hell
challenges you the most?

❖ Which Scripture passage on Hell do you
find the most disturbing, and why?

❖ In 1 Corinthians 6:9–10, St. Paul mentions
certain sins that will prevent someone from
inheriting the kingdom of God. Are there any
sins you struggle with that could send you to
Hell if you do not repent of them? Have you
sought help to overcome this sin? What can you
do to begin to overcome the sin that hinders
most the love that God desires to give you?

❖ Does God's mercy bring you comfort
as you reflect on Hell? If so, how?

3

What the Catholic Church Teaches about Hell

Jesus founded the Catholic Church to transmit and safeguard His teachings until the end of time and, above all, to save souls. After His death, all public revelation ceased.[21] But the revelation and application of Jesus' words given to His apostles and their successors, the popes and the bishops, continues to unfold in the authoritative teachings of the Church's Magisterium. As Jesus declared, "He who hears you hears me, and he who rejects you rejects me, and he who rejects me rejects him who sent me" (Luke 10:16). Since Jesus made Hell a focal point of His teachings in Scripture, His Church must guard and proclaim these same teachings to every generation.

If there is one timeless document that summarizes the key teachings of the Catholic Church, it is the Apostles' Creed. And if there is one line in the Apostles' Creed that affirms the Catholic Church's continual belief in Hell it is this: "He descended into Hell."

The Apostles' Creed is at the heart of what we as Catholics profess. Originating around the second century, the Apostles' Creed

---

[21] Scripture is the highest and most authoritative form of public revelation. It was codified in the Church when the last apostle died and the New Testament was complete. Nothing can be added to or removed from Sacred Scripture.

developed through the centuries and solidified into the form we know today. During Pope Innocent III's papacy (1198–1216), the Apostles' Creed became the official proclamation of the Church. Some scholars believe that each apostle contributed to the creed. The *Catechism of the Catholic Church* (CCC) states: "*The Apostles' Creed is so called because it is rightly considered to be a faithful summary of the apostles' faith. It is the ancient baptismal symbol of the Church of Rome. Its great authority arises from this fact: it is 'the Creed of the Roman Church, the See of Peter the first of the apostles, to which he brought the common faith.'*"[22] (CCC 194). Furthermore, the Apostles' Creed is often referred to as the "oldest Roman catechism" (CCC 196).

What does it mean that Jesus descended into Hell? Because the word *Hell* or the related Hebrew concept of *Sheol* has multiple meanings, different interpretations have ensued as to the exact destination of Jesus' descent. Some argue that Jesus was visiting the "abode of the dead"—where the righteous awaited the Resurrection; others argue that Jesus also visited those in Hell, since Hell has many layers. The early Church saw no contradiction in Jesus' visiting the "abode of the dead" and visiting Hell.[23] It would seem only appropriate that Jesus would descend to the netherworld, since He gave His apostles the Great Commission to "go therefore and make disciples of all nations, baptizing them in the name of the Father and of the Son and of the Holy Spirit" (Matt. 28:19). Jesus wanted the Gospel brought to everyone. Or, as the *Catechism* states,

---

[22] St. Ambrose, Expl. symb. 7: PL 17, 1196.

[23] Msgr. M. Francis Mannion, "What Does It Mean That Jesus Descended into Hell?" Catholic News Agency, February 21, 2017, https://www.catholicnewsagency.com/column/53709/what-does -it-mean-that-jesus-descended-into-Hell.

"The descent into Hell brings the Gospel message of salvation to complete fulfilment"[24] (634).

Despite the differing interpretations regarding the specifics of Jesus' descent into Hell, the *Catechism* states clearly: "Jesus did not descend into hell to deliver the damned, nor to destroy the hell of damnation, but to free the just who had gone before him" (633). The latter point is even more critical than debating whether Jesus set foot in Hell. For if Jesus did not deliver the damned or destroy Hell following His death and even more so after His Resurrection, why would He do it now? Has Jesus somehow changed His mind on the permanence of Hell, or has mankind changed its mind?

The Catholic Church has never wavered on the existence and permanence of Hell: "This state of definitive self-exclusion from communion with God and the blessed is called 'hell'" (CCC 1033).

The *Catechism* further declares:

The teaching of the Church affirms the existence of hell and its eternity. Immediately after death the souls of those who die in a state of mortal sin descend into hell, where they suffer the punishments of hell, "eternal fire."[25] The chief punishment of hell is eternal separation from God, in whom alone man can possess the life and happiness for which he was created and for which he longs. (1035)

When the Catholic Church uses such words as *eternal fire* and *eternal separation*, is she not preaching the same gospel as her

---

[24] Cf. Council of Rome (745): DS 587; Benedict XII, *Cum dudum* (1341): DS 1011; Clement VI, *Super quibusdam* (1351): DS 1077; Council of Toledo IV (625): DS 485; Mt 27:52–53.

[25] Cf. DS 76; 409; 411; 801; 858; 1002; 1351; 1575; Paul VI, CPG § 12.

Founder, Jesus? Is she not echoing the words found throughout the Old and New Testaments? Many will say the Catholic Church is too harsh when it comes to matters of morality, sin, and Hell. The truth is that the Catholic Church is not too harsh; rather, the world and many Christian denominations are too lenient and thus have abandoned the clear teachings of Jesus. They follow a different gospel, one that promises only comfort and leads to total ruin. Interestingly, the greatest pain of the damned is not physical pain, such as "eternal fire," but rather, "eternal separation" from God. We were made for God alone, the fulfillment of all desire and happiness. If we do not end up in Heaven, we will have missed the entire reason for our existence — namely, to love God and to be loved by God forever.

The Catholic Church has convened various councils throughout the centuries to clarify her teachings, especially when heretical beliefs arise. One erroneous belief involved the notion that Hell might not be permanent.[26] Third-century theologian Origen proposed this error, believing that all would be eventually reconciled with God. The Second Council of Constantinople (A.D. 553) condemned this view, declaring the following:

> If anyone says or thinks that the punishment of demons and of impious men is only temporary, and will one day have an end, and that a restoration (ἀποκατάστασις) will take place of demons and of impious men, let him be anathema.
>
> Anathema to Origen and to that Adamantius, who set forth these opinions together with his nefarious and

---

[26] Rev. Francis Spirago, *The Catechism Explained: Newly Annotated with Corresponding References to the Catechism of the Catholic Church*, 273.

execrable and wicked doctrine and to whomsoever there is who thinks thus, or defends these opinions, or in any way hereafter at any time shall presume to protect them.[27]

Keep in mind, Origen was never formally excommunicated from the Catholic Church, though some of his later writings were condemned. In the early Church, the terms *anathema* and *excommunication* had very similar meanings. Specifically, *anathema* "signified the exclusion of a sinner from the society of the faithful; but the anathema was pronounced chiefly against heretics."[28] In fact, the Greek word *anathema* means "a thing cursed," and its Latin derivation means "an excommunicated person; the curse of excommunication."[29] In the sixth century, the terms *anathema* and *excommunication* became distinct.[30] During the pontificate of Pope Gregory IX (1227–1241), the term *anathema* meant a major excommunication with a solemn pontifical ceremony. Because the penalty of anathema was used so rarely, however, it was eventually omitted from the 1983 *Code of Canon Law* and is not part of Church law.[31] Still, the Catholic Church has always taught and will never cease proclaiming that Hell is irreversible. There can be no reconciliation with God, for it is the point of no return. Once a soul enters Hell, he or she can never exit.

---

[27] Second Council of Constantinople, *New Advent*, https://www.newadvent.org/fathers/3812.htm.

[28] Joseph Gignac, "Anathema," *The Catholic Encyclopedia*, vol. 1 (New York: Robert Appleton, 1907), New Advent, https://www.newadvent.org/cathen/01455e.htm.

[29] *Online Etymology Dictionary*, s.v. "anathema," https://www.etymonline.com/search?q=anathema.

[30] Gignac, "Anathema."

[31] Jimmy Akin, "Anathema," *Catholic Answers*, April 1, 2000, https://www.catholic.com/magazine/print-edition/anathema.

Besides the Second Council of Constantinople, two other councils provided definitive statements on Hell. The Second Council of Lyons (1272–1274) declared that "the souls of those who die in mortal sin go at once into Hell."[32] The Council of Florence (1431–1449) said the "punishments in Hell are not all alike,"[33] a topic that will be explored in the next chapter.

In addition to the Church Councils through the years, the *Catechism of the Council of Trent* delivers a powerful and unequivocal stance on Hell. It describes the different abodes called Hell. "These abodes are not all of the same nature, for among them is that most loathsome and dark prison in which the souls of the damned are tormented with the unclean spirits in eternal and inextinguishable fire. This place is called *gehenna*, the bottomless pit, and is Hell strictly so called."[34] Jesus did not descend into Hell to suffer, for He had suffered everything already on the Cross. Jesus came to free the captives of Hell, those righteous souls who lived before and after Him. At the same time, Jesus' power and dignity remained intact.[35]

Even though Jesus' descent into Hell is not recorded in Scripture, we can rely on Sacred Tradition—that which is passed down from the apostles. At the same time, we can only imagine the

---

[32] Rev. Francis Spirago, *The Catechism Explained: Newly Annotated with Corresponding References to the Catechism of the Catholic Church* (Gastonia, NC: TAN Books, 2022), 274.

[33] Spirago, *The Catechism Explained*, 273.

[34] Pope St. Pius V, *The Catechism of the Council of Trent*, 65. The *Catechism of the Council of Trent* was created with St. Charles Borromeo's guidance and with Pope St. Pius V's (1566–1574) approval. It has offered lucidity and instruction in the Faith for more than four hundred years, even with the latest *Catechism*.

[35] *Catechism of the Council of Trent*, 66.

scene of Jesus meeting Satan in Hell—one of the greatest events not recorded in Scripture but revealed through a vision of Bl. Anne Catherine Emmerich.[36] The Catholic Church does not definitively say who is in Hell with the exception of the fallen angels. Several Doctors of the Church, such as St. Augustine, St. Thomas Aquinas, and St. Alphonsus Liguori, believed that Judas is in Hell. They argue that Judas despaired of God's mercy and thus refused to accept His grace.

We must never forget that God wishes Hell for no one, not even the greatest heretics and sinners. Jesus did not die the most horrific and painful death so that souls would be lost. No, He died so that souls would be saved from Hell, and He always seeks out the one lost sheep, leaving behind the other ninety-nine (see Matt. 18:12–14; Luke 15:3–7). The beautiful words from St. Matthew's Gospel reveal the Father's will that everyone make it to Heaven: "So it is not the will of my Father who is in heaven that one of these little ones should perish" (18:14).

The *Catechism* reiterates Jesus' desire to save souls, not to condemn them:

> God predestines no one to go to hell;[37] for this, a willful turning away from God (a mortal sin) is necessary, and persistence in it until the end. In the Eucharistic liturgy and in the daily prayers of her faithful, the Church implores the mercy of God, who does not want "any to perish, but all to come to repentance" (2 Pet. 3:9). (1037)

---

[36] Bl. Anne Catherine Emmerich, *The Dolorous Passion of Our Lord Jesus Christ* (Charlotte, NC: TAN Books, 2012), 347.

[37] Cf. Council of Orange II (529):DS 397; Council of Trent (1547): 1567.

The Truth about Hell

In his General Audience on July 28, 1999, Pope St. John Paul reinforced the Church's teachings on Hell, reminding us that Hell is ultimately man's choosing, not God's doing:

> "Eternal damnation", therefore, is not attributed to God's initiative because in his merciful love he can only desire the salvation of the beings he created. In reality, it is the creature who closes himself to his love. Damnation consists precisely in definitive separation from God, freely chosen by the human person and confirmed with death that seals his choice for ever. God's judgement ratifies this state.

Notice the phrases "freely chosen" and "seals his choice for ever." Once a person crosses the threshold of death, his fate for all eternity remains—there is no turning back. The gates are locked from within—locked by the person's free choice to reject God and His honoring that choice. Although the choice of Hell is final, this decision was not made once but entailed a lifetime of choosing evil over good, sin over virtue, as Pope St. John Paul II's successor, Pope Benedict XVI, declared in his papal encyclical *Spe Salvi*, or "Saved in Hope":

> With death, our life-choice becomes definitive—our life stands before the judge. Our choice, which in the course of an entire life takes on a certain shape, can have a variety of forms. There can be people who have totally destroyed their desire for truth and readiness to love, people for whom everything has become a lie, people who have lived for hatred and have suppressed all love within themselves. This is a terrifying thought, but alarming profiles of this type can be seen in certain figures of our own history. In such people all would be beyond remedy and the destruction

of good would be irrevocable: this is what we mean by the word *Hell.*[38]

Before our current *Catechism*, with its many references to Hell, was promulgated by Pope St. John Paul II in 1992, another saintly pope, St. Pius X (r. 1903–1914) wrote his own catechism for the laity. Article 7 of the *Catechism of Pope Pius X* draws our attention particularly to the following line from the Apostles' Creed: "From thence He shall come to judge the living and the dead." This article refers to Jesus' Final Judgment, or in the words of Pope Pius X's catechism:

> The Seventh Article of the Creed teaches us that at the end of the world Jesus Christ, in all His glory and majesty, will come from heaven to judge all men, both good and bad, and to give each of them the reward or the punishment he shall have merited.

At the moment of death, each of us will undergo a particular judgment by God. We will then enter either Heaven, Hell, or Purgatory. At the end of time, the Final Judgment will occur, when our souls will be reunited with our bodies. The Final Judgment will confirm each person's particular judgment. The good (who have been made good by the sacrifice of Jesus and their embrace of that sacrifice) will receive their reward, while the bad (those who have rejected the gift of Jesus' sacrifice and desire a life apart from God) will be given what they have desired and have lived for all eternity. Death, judgment, Hell, and Heaven are frequently referred to as the Four Last Things. These are not the only last things but the

---

[38] Pope Benedict XVI, encyclical letter *Spe Salvi* (November 30, 2007), no. 45.

four most important things. As seen throughout history, especially in her councils, catechisms, and papal documents, the Catholic Church has a mission to bring as many souls to Heaven as possible by never wavering from speaking on these hard truths.

Most parents have eighteen years to form their children before those children leave home for the "real world." In that time, parents must do everything in their power to teach their children the Faith, right from wrong, and various skills and training to help them thrive as adults. In the same manner, the Catholic Church has a short window to remind us of what awaits us on the other side of the veil. The Catholic Church is our Mother, and she must instruct us and keep us on the narrow way that leads to Heaven, disciplining us and calling us back when we stray.

The Catholic Church is also the hospital of sinners. She knows we are weak and sinful, so she offers the sacraments — through the love and sacrifice of Jesus — to heal us and strengthen us. She gives us the writings of her saints, especially the Doctors of the Church, to provide particular medicines for our spiritual ailments. Finally, the Catholic Church is the instrument of salvation with Jesus as her source. And those who take refuge in Jesus and His Catholic Church, the ark of salvation, will find shelter from the powers of Hell and eternal perdition.

Questions for Reflection

❖ What stood out, struck you, or
moved you in this chapter?

❖ How can you reconcile the Church's
teaching on Hell with God's infinite mercy?

❖ Have you ever found any of the Catholic
Church's teachings very challenging, especially
her teaching on Hell? If so, why?

❖ Do you find it difficult to accept the teaching
that Hell is permanent? Why or why not?

❖ What is all of this understanding leading you
to with respect to how you live out your Faith?

4

The Doctors of the Church on Hell

Nicknamed the "golden tongue" for his elegant preaching, St. John Chrysostom (347–407) is often credited with the following words: "The road to Hell is paved with the bones of priests and monks, and the skulls of bishops are the lampposts that light the path." It seems that an original source has never been identified for this quote, making it possible that he never uttered such words.[39] Regardless, an important point must be made. Hell does not care what your vocation is or even if you are Catholic. Hell welcomes everyone. In particular, Hell loves it when we sin and drag others with us down its slippery path. Furthermore, Hell rejoices over one sinner who is lost, especially if that sinner is a priest or a religious. That is why St. John Chrysostom—a Doctor of the Church—and so many other saints preached and wrote on the Four Last Things. They, like Jesus, did not want others to end up in Hell; above all, *they* did not want to end up in Hell.

At present, the Catholic Church has thirty-six Doctors.[40] The Church does not freely bestow the title "Doctor" on any saint; it

---

[39] Trent Horn, "Is the Road to Hell Paved with the Skulls of Priests?" *Catholic Answers*, September 5, 2018, https://www.catholic.com/magazine/online-edition/is-the-road-to-Hell-paved-with-the-skulls-of-priests.

[40] Here is a list of the thirty-six Doctors of the Church in the order they received the title: St. Ambrose (1298), St. Augustine of

is a highly formal process requiring a papal declaration. These thirty-six saints have distinguished themselves by their sanctity and by their contributions to theology or doctrine. First used in the thirteenth-century by Pope Boniface VIII on four saints—Gregory the Great, Ambrose, Augustine, and Jerome—"Doctor" is one of the greatest titles the Catholic Church can bestow on a saint. It does not mean that every word these saints wrote was without error; rather, it means that these saints can be trusted. Their writings and holiness of life are sound.

To research and list what every Doctor of the Church wrote on Hell could take years and would consume many volumes. Hence, this chapter will focus on the more prominent Doctors. As seen in previous chapters, Jesus and the Catholic Church have definitively affirmed that Hell is real and permanent. The writings of the Doctors further illuminate these teachings.

Before his conversion to the Catholic Church, St. Augustine of Hippo, by his choice, lived a life contrary to the offer and call of

---

Hippo (1298), St. Jerome (1298), St. Gregory the Great (1298), St. Athanasius (1298), St. John Chrysostom (1568), St. Basil the Great (1568), St. Gregory of Nazianzus (1568), St. Thomas Aquinas (1568), St. Bonaventure (1588), St. Anselm of Canterbury (1720), St. Isidore of Seville (1722), St. Peter Chrysologus (1729), St. Leo the Great (1754), St. Peter Damian (1828), St. Bernard of Clairvaux (1830), St. Hilary of Potiers (1851), St. Alphonsus Liguori (1871), St. Francis de Sales (1877), St. Cyril of Alexandria (1882), St. Cyril of Jerusalem (1882), St. John Damascene (1890), St. Bede the Venerable (1899), St. Ephrem the Syrian (1920), St. Peter Canisius (1925), St. John of the Cross (1926), St. Robert Bellarmine (1931), St. Albert the Great (1932), St. Anthony of Padua (1946), St. Lawrence of Brindisi (1959), Saint Teresa of Avila (1970), St. Catherine of Siena (1970), St. Thérèse of Lisieux (1997), St. John of Avila (2012), St. Hildegard of Bingen (2012), and St. Gregory of Narek (2015).

God and thus worthy of Hell. He fathered a child out of wedlock; he stole; he engaged in debauchery. He was no friend of God. In his masterpiece autobiography, *Confessions*, St. Augustine admitted that he was on the path to perdition: "And lo, there was I received by the scourge of bodily sickness, and I was going down to Hell, carrying all the sins which I had committed, both against Thee, and myself, and others, many and grievous, over and above that bond of original sin, *whereby we all die in Adam*."[41] Without the persistent prayers of his mother, St. Monica, which helped him recover physically and eventually spiritually, St. Augustine would have departed into the "fire and torments" that his "misdeeds deserved."[42] He is said to have written *Confessions*, arguably the most famous autobiography in history, around A.D. 396 to 400. Roughly between 413 and 426, he wrote another timeless piece, *The City of God*. More than a thousand pages long and comprising twenty-two books, *The City of God* defends Christianity against a pagan world, especially following the fall of Rome in 410. In this volume, St. Augustine touched on the most essential themes of our Faith, Hell being among them. Writing on the fallen angels, St. Augustine declares the following:

> For, though a life never be so long, it cannot be truly called eternal life if it is destined to have an end; for it is called life inasmuch as it is lived, but eternal because it has no end. Wherefore, although everything eternal is not therefore blessed (for hell-fire is eternal), yet if no life can be truly and perfectly blessed except it [that blessedness] be eternal, the life of these angels was not blessed, for it [their blessedness]

---

[41] *Confessions of St. Augustine* (Boston: E. P. Peabody, 1842), 76.
[42] *Confessions*, 77.

was doomed to end, and therefore not eternal, whether they knew it or not. In the one case fear, in other ignorance, prevented them from being blessed.[43]

St. Augustine was clear: "Hell-fire is eternal." The fires of Hell never stop because eternity has no end. For a period, all of the angels enjoyed some blessedness. Like us, they were given an opportunity to serve God or not to serve Him. But when many of them (one-third) rebelled against God, their "blessedness was destined to come to an end."[44] And it is the same for us: whatever blessedness we experience in this passing life will give way either to the Beatific Vision of perpetual blessedness in Heaven or to the absence of such in perpetual darkness in Hell. Only Jesus offers eternal life. "And this is eternal life, that they know thee the only true God, and Jesus Christ whom thou hast sent" (John 17:3). Only Satan offers eternal death.

During St. Augustine's time (354–430), many "tender-hearted Christians,"[45] as he liked to call them, believed that eternal punishment did not exist. Recall that Origen, about a century earlier, erroneously believed that men and demons would not suffer eternally. Eventually, he thought, God would have mercy on them. If there was one saint who knew God's mercy and would seem the most sympathetic to Origen's claim, it would have been St. Augustine. And yet St. Augustine stood firm in his convictions about Hell, because he was an authentic disciple of Christ and His Church. St. Augustine, as much as any saint, knew how much his sins and others wounded Christ.

---

43 *The City of God*, trans. Marcus Dods (New York: Hafner Publishing), vol. 1, 450–451.

44 *City of God*, vol. 1, 452.

45 *City of God*, vol. 2, 444.

Citing Scripture throughout *The City of God*, St. Augustine reinforced the teaching of Jesus and the Church that Hell is permanent and involves torment. Specifically, St. Augustine wrote, "And to say in one and the same sense, life eternal shall be endless, punishment eternal shall come to an end, is the height of absurdity. Wherefore, as the eternal life of the saints shall be endless, so too the eternal punishment of those who are doomed to it shall have no end."[46] Indeed, St. Augustine saw the absurdity in the claim that only Heaven is eternal, while Hell is temporary. He also noted how the "spirit, whose presence animates and rules the body, can both suffer pain and cannot die. Here then is something which, though it can feel pain, is immortal. And this capacity, which we now see in the spirit of all, shall be hereafter in the bodies of the damned."[47] In other words, both the soul and the body will suffer forever, especially when they are reunited at the resurrection of the dead.

At the same time, some argued that it is impossible for a body to be eternally consumed by fire. St. Augustine cited things in nature, such as diamonds, to prove that not everything is consumed by fire. While Scripture is often silent when it comes to the "spiritual pain of the damned," according to St. Augustine, he noted that "in a body thus tormented the soul also is tortured with a fruitless repentance."[48] He also held that "one fire shall be the lot of both [demons and man], for thus the truth has declared."[49] The truth is not something, but Someone: Jesus. And Jesus Christ has revealed that Hell is a "lake of fire and brimstone" (Rev. 20:10).

46 *City of God*, vol. 2, 451.
47 *City of God*, vol. 2, 415–416.
48 *City of God*, vol. 2, 433.
49 *City of God*, vol. 2, 436.

Describing the Final Judgment, St. Augustine added, "For that day is properly called the day of judgment, because in it there shall be no room left for the ignorant questioning why this wicked person is happy and that righteous man unhappy. In that day true and full happiness shall be the lot of none but the good, while deserved and supreme misery shall be the portion of the wicked, and of them only."[50] St. Augustine's words evoke the parable of the rich man and Lazarus. Eternal happiness awaits the just man, while eternal misery awaits the unjust.

St. Augustine further believed that each one of us deserves Hell for our sins: "No one is exempt from this just and due punishment," that is, "unless delivered by mercy and underserved grace."[51] The question remains: Why doesn't God show mercy to everyone by saving them from Hell? St. Augustine answers as follows:

> If all had been transferred from darkness to light, the severity of retribution would have been manifested in none. But many more are left under punishment than are delivered from it, in order that it may thus be shown what was due to all. And had it been inflicted on all, no one could justly have found fault with the justice of Him who taketh vengeance; whereas, in the deliverance of so many from that just award, there is cause to render the most cordial thanks to the gratuitous bounty of Him who delivers.[52]

If God showed mercy to every soul in Hell by emptying it, then His justice would not be glorified, and if He showed only justice, then His mercy would not be glorified. God, indeed, shows mercy

---

50 *City of God*, vol. 2, 346.
51 *City of God*, vol. 2, 438.
52 *City of God*, vol. 2, 438.

to every soul, and most refuse it in their lives, especially at the hour of death. One thing is clear: had mercy and truth not found St. Augustine, he would have, by his own admission, marched into Hell.

St. Augustine was one of the first Doctors of the Church to write extensively on Hell, but he was not the last. His writings have influenced great sinners and great saints, one being St. Thomas Aquinas. In his *Summa Theologiae*, St. Thomas Aquinas quotes St. Augustine more than any other saint. Written from 1265 to 1273, more than eight hundred years after St. Augustine's death, the *Summa Theologiae* continues where St. Augustine left off regarding the punishment of the damned. St. Thomas poses the following seven questions concerning Hell and then systematically answers each of them: Whether in Hell the damned are tormented by the sole punishment of fire? Whether the worm of the damned is corporeal? Whether the weeping of the damned will be corporeal? Whether the damned are in material darkness? Whether the fire of Hell will be corporeal? Whether the fire of Hell is of the same species as ours? Whether the fire of Hell is beneath the earth?[53] Clearly, St. Thomas believed that Hell is real. His beliefs were grounded in Sacred Scripture and Sacred Tradition, including wisdom from those Doctors of the Church who preceded him. For instance, St. Thomas stated the following:

> Whatever we may say of the fire that torments the separated souls, we must admit that the fire which will torment the bodies of the damned after the resurrection is corporeal, since one cannot fittingly apply a punishment to a body unless that punishment itself be bodily. Wherefore Gregory

---

[53] *The Summa Theologiae of St. Thomas Aquinas* (*ST*), 2nd rev. ed., trans. Fathers of the English Dominican Province (1920), New Advent, https://www.newadvent.org/summa/.

(*Dial.* iv) proves the fire of Hell to be corporeal from the very fact that the wicked will be cast thither after the resurrection. Again Augustine, as quoted in the text of *Sentent.* iv, D, 44, clearly admits (*De Civ. Dei* xxi, 10) that the fire by which the bodies are tormented is corporeal. And this is the point at issue for the present. We have said elsewhere (Supplement, 70, 3) how the souls of the damned are punished by this corporeal fire.[54]

The fires of the Hell are meant to be taken literally, and they will burn the bodies of the damned after the resurrection of the dead. In another point, St. Thomas argued that the fires of Hell are of the same species as the fires we have on earth, though we don't know for sure "whether it subsists in its proper matter, or if it subsists in a strange matter."[55] In other words, the fire of Hell resembles earthly fire in its nature, properties, and characteristics (such as burning, heat, etc.). But St. Thomas acknowledged that it is not known whether it is of the same material (or physical and chemical composition) as earthly fire. He pointed out, for example, that the fire of Hell does not require fuel to continue burning, whereas earthly fire does. St. Thomas believed that the fires of Hell will be of the greatest intensity. St. Anselm and St. Alphonsus Liguori also declared that the fires of Hell surpass any earthly fire, for the former is meant solely for punishment while the latter is for man's use.[56] St. Thomas believed that the punishments are as "various as the sins committed on earth; they depend on the nature, number, and gravity of the sin."[57]

[54] *ST*, Supplement, q. 97.
[55] *ST*, Supplement, q. 97.
[56] *Sermons of St. Alphonsus Liguori*, 90.
[57] Spirago, *The Catechism Explained*, 273.

Regarding bodies burning in Hell, St. Bonaventure said that "if the body of one of the damned were placed in the Earth, it would, by its stench, be sufficient to cause the death of all men."[58] Now multiply that stench by the many souls for all eternity, and you will have touched on one of the greatest torments in Hell, not to mention the physical pain of fire. These torments and others will be explored more deeply in the next chapter, concerning the saints' visions of Hell.

In the *Summa Theologiae*, St. Thomas poses the question of whether Hell is beneath the earth. Keep in mind, Hell exists both as a place and as a state. Citing St. Augustine and St. Gregory the Great, he declares the following:

> As Augustine says (*De Civ. Dei* xv, 16), "I am of opinion that no one knows in what part of the world Hell is situated, unless the Spirit of God has revealed this to some one." Wherefore Gregory (*Dial.* iv) having been questioned on this point answers: "About this matter I dare not give a rash decision. For some have deemed Hell to be in some part of the earth's surface; others think it to be beneath the earth."[59]

Despite the mystery of Hell's location, St. Thomas believed, based on Scripture, that Hell is beneath the earth. Ultimately, the Doctors of the Church, such as St. John Chrysostom, believed that it is more important to avoid Hell than to find out where it is.[60]

Another Doctor and one of the Church's greatest biblical schol-ars is St. Bede the Venerable, an eighth-century Benedictine monk

---

[58] Spirago, *The Catechism Explained*, 83.
[59] ST, Supplement, q. 97.
[60] Spirago, *The Catechism Explained*, 271.

The Truth about Hell

who vividly described Hell. Specifically, he wrote a powerful poem
on Hell called "On the Day of Judgment":

> Alas, what woes
> Lost souls await!
> What torments dire
> Of fiery fate
> The netherworld
> Of Hell may hold!
> Grim paradox—
> That heat and cold
> Together both
> At once combine,
> Corrosive, sharp
> As fuller's lime.
>
> And demon hordes
> Of gruesome mien
> And hideous heart
> Shall therein teem,
> With tridents armed
> And red-hot brands,
> Which clasp they firm
> In rugged hands,
> With which untold
> Pains they inflict.
> Thus ruthlessly
> They so afflict
>
> The bodies, souls
> And minds of those
> Who, sin-deceived,

> The wide path chose,
> With agonies
> Without release,
> Never to end,
> Never to cease.[61]

Hot, cold, pain, agony, and *torment* are just a few of the terms St. Bede used to refer to the never-ending place known as Hell. All of these descriptors reinforce what Jesus and other Doctors of the Church have warned us about Hell.

St. Jerome writes: "In one fire, sinners will feel all the torments in Hell."[62] Every pain we face on earth will be present in Hell, especially sufferings in our bodies and in our souls. And these earthly torments are nothing compared with what the damned experience, according to St. John Chrysostom.[63]

St. Alphonsus Liguori preached and wrote comprehensively on the topic of Hell. Living in the eighteenth century, this Italian bishop worked tirelessly to ensure that none of his flock ended up in Hell. He offers a vivid description of the sufferings there: "This fire shall torment the damned not only externally, but also internally. It will burn the bowels, the heart, the brains, the blood within the veins, and the marrow within the bones. The skin of the damned shall be like a caldron, in which their bowels, their flesh, and their bones shall be burned."[64] As painful as this sounds, physical torments are only one form of punishment. St. Alphonsus

---

[61] The original is "Hymnus de Die Judicii" (Hymn on the Day of Judgment), trans. Fr. Robert Nixon, O.S.B.

[62] "In uno igne omnia supplicia sentient in inferno peccatores." Quoted in *Sermons of St. Alphonsus*, 92.

[63] *Ep. ad Pam*, quoted in *Sermons of St. Alphonsus*, 94.

[64] *Sermons of St. Alphonsus*, 91.

described the remorse of the damned, such as how easy it would have been to save their souls, the remembrance of all the gifts God gave them, and how they forfeited Heaven over a few fleeting pleasures. St. Peter Chrysologus, a fifth-century Italian bishop said it best about the pain of the damned: "He is tormented more by heaven than by hell."[65] On earth, many people are tormented by regret. Perhaps it is the regret of a past sin or a failed relationship. These regrets can disturb our peace, sometimes for years. Hell is never-ending regret.

Of all the pains experienced in Hell, the greatest is the loss of the Beatific Vision. Or, as the twelfth-century Benedictine monk and archbishop of Canterbury St. Anselm said, "the worst of all the multitude of the punishments and torments which shall afflict the condemned is the knowledge that they have been deprived, forever and definitively, of the glory of the vision of God."[66]

Since God is infinite, the soul who loses God will experience infinite loss. Imagine losing something valuable on earth, such as a favorite rosary or a prized ring; now compound that loss by infinity. Hence, the minds of the damned will be tormented by constant remorse. They need not the demons to remind them of what they have lost, though God will certainly use them as His instruments.

Jesus says that, in Hell, "men will weep and gnash their teeth" (Matt. 8:12). What is the cause of the damned souls' constant weeping? According to St. Alphonsus, "it is the thought of having lost God through their own fault."[67] They have forfeited the

---

[65] "Plus coelo torquetur, quam Gehenna." *Sermons of St. Alphonsus*, 82.

[66] St. Anselm of Canterbury, *The Glories of Heaven: The Supernatural Gifts That Await Body and Soul in Paradise*, trans. Fr. Robert Nixon, O.S.B. (Gastonia, NC: TAN Books, 2022), 70.

[67] St. Anselm of Canterbury, *The Glories of Heaven*, 361.

highest good, God Himself, for such trifling pleasures and vices. And there is no hope in Hell because those souls will *never* be reunited with God. One million years from now, they will still be burning in pain and weeping in their misery. And unlike in Heaven, where the sight of others brings joy, the other souls in Hell will only increase one's misery.

But that is not the end of it. The damned souls will see how much Jesus suffered for them and have now lost His love. Since they cannot love God anymore, they hate him. Or, in the words of St. Alphonsus, "their Hell consists in hating God whom they at the same time know to be infinitely amiable."[68] They have joined the opposing team: Satan and his minions. And now, in the fullest way possible, they hate everything that is of God, especially the sacraments and God's saints and angels. Hell is unending hate, pain, regret, and sorrow.

In the fourteenth century, St. Catherine of Siena had several mystical experiences from God, which are recorded in her book *The Dialogue of St. Catherine of Siena.* Concerning the torments of the damned, God the Father told her that the "tongue is not sufficient to narrate the pain of these poor souls."[69] Specifically, God told St. Catherine that the souls in Hell experience four main torments. The first involves being prevented from seeing God. The second is that their conscience "gnaws unceasingly" at them.[70] The third is the vision of the devil. Yes, instead of the Beatific Vision, they see the diabolical vision. St. Catherine says that the sight of the

---

[68] St. Anselm of Canterbury, *The Glories of* Heaven, 367.

[69] *The Dialogue of St. Catherine of Siena: A Conversation with God on Living Your Spiritual Life to the Fullest* (Charlotte, NC: TAN Books, 2010), 54.

[70] *Dialogue,* 54.

devil is unimaginable. And the fourth torture is the fire that God allows "according to the diversity of their sins."[71] And these four torments lead to all other sufferings in Hell.

Why such torment, we might ask? God made it clear to St. Catherine that Hell is ultimately man's choosing: "Now because they did not amend themselves after the first reproof that they had of injustice and false judgment, neither in the second, which was that, in death, they would not hope in Me, nor grieve for the offense done to Me, but only for their own pain, have they thus miserably received eternal punishment."[72] God also told St. Catherine that Judas' despair hurt Him more than his betrayal.

In the spiritual life, many souls, especially the saints, have tasted Hell. When we sin, we all experience a firsthand touch of Hell. Our sins also create a foretaste of Hell for other people, for there is no such thing as a private sin. During the "dark night of the soul," a term coined by St. John of the Cross, "when this purgative contemplation oppresses a man, he feels very vividly indeed the shadow of death, the sighs of death, and the sorrows of Hell, all of which reflect the feeling of God's absence, of being chastised and rejected by Him, and of being unworthy of Him, as well as the object of His anger. The soul experiences all this and even more, for now it seems that this affliction will last forever."[73] God wills that certain souls be stripped of everything in this life, even His very presence, so as to cling to Him in deeper faith. Did not Jesus experience a similar trial, the greatest desolation, on the Cross? All of Hell unleased its fury on Good Friday, and all of Hell will unleash its fury on our deathbed.

[71] *Dialogue*, 55.
[72] *Dialogue*, 55.
[73] *Collected Works*, 338.

In *The Story of a Soul*, one of the most renowned autobiographies after St. Augustine's *Confessions*, St. Thérèse of Lisieux recounts the tale of a vicious criminal who would have ended up in Hell save for a miracle. His name was Henri Pranzini, and he was convicted of killing three women in Paris. St. Thérèse says, "I wanted at all costs to prevent him from falling into Hell, and to attain my purpose I employed every means imaginable."[74] St. Thérèse asked her sister Céline to have a Mass offered for Henri's conversion. Together, they prayed fervently for this intention. St. Thérèse felt certain that God would answer her prayer and even asked for a sign. And she received that sign: right before Henri's execution, he kissed Jesus' sacred wounds three times on the crucifix a priest held out to him.

The Doctors of the Church repeatedly warn us that Hell exists and must be avoided at all costs. As seen throughout this chapter, their writings reiterate what has been stated in Sacred Scripture and Sacred Tradition. Though we know Hell is real, questions about its location and specific pains remain a mystery. For these details, we will explore accounts from saints who saw or even visited Hell.

---

[74] *The Story of a Soul: The Autobiography of Saint Thérèse of Lisieux*, 3rd ed., trans. John Clarke, O.C.D. (Washington, D.C.: ICS Publications, 1996), 99.

Questions for Reflection

❖ What stood out, struck you, or
moved you in this chapter?

❖ St. Augustine said it is absurd to think that
Heaven is perpetual but Hell shall come to an
end. Why do you think Hell must never end?

❖ Which punishment of Hell described
by the Doctors of the Church terrifies
you the most, and why?

❖ Do you pray for the conversion of sinners? If
so, have you seen any fruit from this practice?

5

Saints Who Saw Hell

—◇—

The saints spent their lives not only drawing souls to God but also warning sinners about Hell, even making reparation for sin. Since the saints were the closest people to God, they knew how much the smallest sin wounds Him. Throughout Church history, several saints had visions of Hell, and some were literally taken to Hell. These horrifying experiences led them to recommit their lives to Christ and to do everything in their power to pray and to offer sacrifices for the conversion of sinners. It is no secret that Satan hates the saints. For one, they wrest sinners from his clutches. And second, the saints take the place of the fallen angels in Heaven.

As alluded to earlier, several saints, such as Alphonsus Liguori, Teresa of Avila, and John of the Cross believed, as Jesus taught in Matthew 7:14, that more souls will be lost than saved. Our Lady of Fatima conveys a similar message. Some have even been taken to Hell. Although several saints saw Hell and Satan, this chapter will focus on just a handful of accounts.

St. Padre Pio

When St. Padre Pio was asked what he thought of those who denied Hell's existence, he replied, "They will very well believe in

Hell when they get there."[75] St. Padre Pio could say that Hell existed because he had personally experienced Hell. Padre Benedetto, St. Padre Pio's spiritual father, said the following:

> Padre Pio has experienced the torments of Hell in seeing the damned suffer. About two years ago [this refers to 1919] every ten or fifteen days he underwent this agony. He felt the pains of the senses and of damnation, finding himself in body and soul amongst the damned and the demons, in order to save others and himself from that place where they were destined if grace had not helped them.[76]

St. Padre Pio believed wholeheartedly that Hell exists. He would often warn sinners that Hell could be their final lot if they did not repent. For instance, a man found out that his girlfriend was pregnant with his child, and the girlfriend's father pressured the man into marrying her (the man literally felt her father's shotgun digging into his back). But after they married and the baby was born, the husband left his wife and young son for his mistress. Surprisingly, the man took his mistress to San Giovanni in hopes that St. Padre Pio would approve of his decision. St. Pio was very gentle with him, but told him in no uncertain terms that he had to return to his wife and be there for his son. Specifically, he said to the man, "You must return to your child."[77]

---

[75] "Stories of Hell in the Lives of the Saints," Mystics of the Church, https://www.mysticsofthechurch.com/2013/03/stories-of-hell-in-lives-of-saints.html.

[76] Padre Benedetto Nardella's "Notes on Padre Pio," quoted in C. Bernard Ruffin, *Padre Pio: The True Story* (Huntington, IN: Our Sunday Visitor, 2018), 340.

[77] Mary O'Regan, "Dónal Enright, a Witness to Many Miracles of Padre Pio, When Padre Pio Lived on This Earth, and Now as St. Pio

While he did not mention the word *Hell*, he interceded for the man to be given a very strong interior warning that he was on his way to Hell if he did not repent and return to his wife and his young son. St. Padre Pio told him that his salvation was in danger. The man left his mistress and begged for his wife's forgiveness. And the man was much happier and better off for listening to St. Padre Pio. The man was also content for his story to be known, with his name withheld: that he had been on the way to Hell before St. Padre Pio had commanded him to return to his wife. Also, during this visit, St. Padre Pio did not absolve the unfaithful husband, but later, when he came back, after he had reunited with his wife, Pio absolved him, and the man was seen to be extremely joyful.[78]

St. Frances of Rome

From 1430 to 1434, St. Frances of Rome had visions of Hell, Purgatory, and Heaven. This devout wife, mother, and Benedictine oblate (third order Benedictine) was shown many things that startled her, especially about Hell. St. Frances described the gates of Hell and its foreboding inscription that read with dark crimson lettering the following:

> Behold, this place is Hell,
> Where souls condemned must dwell.
> Of all the lands accursed
> This is by far the worst!
> From pain there is no rest

Intercedes for Us from His Heavenly Home," Mary's Blog, September 24, 2010, https://thepathlesstaken7.blogspot.com/2010/09/donal-enright-witness-to-many-miracles_24.html.
[78] O'Regan, "Dónal Enright."

Within these realms unblessed:
The flames here burn forever,
The torment ceases never![79]

God showed St. Frances the torments that corresponded with the various sins, especially the seven deadly sins. No one can conceive of the horror and humiliation that awaits those who die in mortal sin without repentance. For those guilty of lust, a demon will torture them with its slobbery tongue, licking them repeatedly with its "vicious and acidic saliva."[80] She also saw the various punishments for other sins, such as vanity, gossip, and dishonoring one's parents. Those who betrayed the Catholic Church (apostates and schismatics) also had severe punishments. God revealed to St. Frances the specific torments for corrupt prelates. Indeed, bishops, abbots, cardinals, and even popes were present in Hell. Seated in chairs suspended in the air by ropes and representing their episcopal thrones and wearing fiery helmets to represent miters, these prelates were assaulted by a ravenous wolf below. As they say, the punishment fits the crime.

St. Frances said that Hell is divided into three levels (lowest, middle, and uppermost) where various demons reside according to their former rank in Heaven. The fallen angels of the highest choirs—the seraphim, the cherubim, and the thrones—occupy the lowest and darkest regions of Hell.[81] This makes sense, as the devil and Hell are inversions of God and Heaven. Those fallen angels who once had the highest positions in the angelic rank are

---

[79] *The Visions of Saint Frances of Rome: Hell, Purgatory, and Heaven Revealed*, trans. Fr. Robert Nixon, O.S.B. (Gastonia, NC: TAN Books, 2023), 17.

[80] *Visions of Saint Frances*, 55.

[81] *Visions of Saint Frances*, 79.

now the least in Hell. Those who were set to be the closest to the throne of God are now the furthest away. The first shall be last (see Mark 10:31)!

While God's presence pervades everywhere, even in Hell, it is Satan who permeates all three levels of Hell, spewing fire and stench. St. Frances described the devil as "utterly terrifying" with his "sinister tiara" and multiple horns.[82] The sounds of wailing and crying and blasphemies led her to shed tears of sorrow. One final point worth mentioning is that there are two demons assigned to every soul in Hell, according to St. Frances. One demon inflicts punishment, while the other one reminds the damned soul of its transgressions and omissions.

St. Teresa of Avila

One century after St. Frances of Rome lived, St. Teresa of Avila was born in Spain. St. Teresa entered the Carmelite Order at the age of twenty, living a very lax religious life. She would often spend more time in the parlor speaking to wealthy guests than in mental prayer—that is, until the Lord revealed to her her place in Hell. In her autobiography, she describes her horrifying vision:

> I was one day in prayer when I found myself in a moment, without knowing how, plunged apparently into Hell. I understood that it was our Lord's will I should see the place which the devils kept in readiness for me, and which I had deserved by my sins. It was but a moment, but it seems to me impossible I should ever forget it, even if I were to live many years.

---

[82] *Visions of Saint Frances*, 20.

The entrance seemed to be by a long narrow pass, like a furnace, very low, dark, and close. The ground seemed to be saturated with water, mere mud, exceedingly foul, sending forth pestilential odours, and covered with loathsome vermin. At the end was a hollow place in the wall, like a closet, and in that I saw myself confined. All this was even pleasant to behold in comparison with what I felt there. There is no exaggeration in what I am saying.[83]

St. Teresa called her bodily sufferings "unendurable."[84] She also said that all of her sufferings on earth, which were substantial, still could not begin to match the amount of pain she experienced in Hell. Her soul was literally being ripped apart. She described the "inward fire and despair" as the greatest sufferings of all. God showed mercy on St. Teresa through this vision, even though, years later, this experience would still frighten her. Her terrifying vision called her not to fear suffering in this life, especially persecutions that might arise. But even more importantly, she began to live her vocation with renewed vigor as she sought to follow her rule perfectly and avoid all sin. She began making reparation for her sins as well as the sins of others. Seeing the torments of Hell led St. Teresa to a massive conversion of heart, and the Lord provides the witness of Scripture and the saints so that we, too, might be warned to flee to His merciful love.

It must be pointed out that St. Teresa was not living a wicked life. She had dedicated her life to God as a cloistered religious and was receiving the sacraments. Her vision of Hell ought to be a warning to each of us. If the cloister walls do not guarantee

---

[83] *The Autobiography of St. Teresa of Avila*, trans. David Lewis (Charlotte, NC: TAN Books, 2012), 288–299.

[84] *Autobiography of St. Teresa*, 299.

Heaven, what of the fate of the laity? Finally, St. Teresa was also distressed at the sight of so many lost souls. How often do we pray for the dying? On average, roughly 116 people die per minute, 6,952 die per hour, and 166,859 die per day worldwide. In the United States, more than 300 people die per hour and 8,000 per day.[85] Who is praying for these souls?

St. John Bosco

Born three hundred years after St. Teresa of Avila, in 1815, St. John Bosco was an Italian priest who founded the Society of St. Francis de Sales and devoted his life to assisting impoverished boys. Beginning at the age of nine, he had vision-like dreams throughout his life. Like St. Frances of Rome, he saw in a vision the gates of Hell, which bore the inscription *Ubi non est redemptio*, or "The place of no reprieve."[86] He also saw various Scripture passages on bronze portals throughout Hell. These passages were Jesus' words pertaining to Hell. St. John Bosco mentioned Hell's intense heat, flames, and smoke.

In the same dream, St. John Bosco saw one of his spiritual sons running in haste to Hell, literally falling into a ravine as he looked back in horror. When the saint inquired about the boy's expression of terror, he heard: "Because God's wrath will pierce Hell's gates to reach and torment him even in the midst of fire!"[87]

[85] "How Many People Die Each Day in 2024?" World Population Review, https://worldpopulationreview.com/countries/deaths -per-day.

[86] St. John Bosco, *Forty Dreams of St. John Bosco, the Apostle of Youth: From the Biographical Memoirs of St. John Bosco* (Charlotte, NC: TAN Books, 2014), 152.

[87] *Forty Dreams*, 153.

He saw other boys falling into Hell with their specific sins written on their foreheads. Specifically, St. John Bosco learned that "*bad companions, bad books, and bad habits*"[88] were what led many souls to Hell. St. John Bosco's dream did not end there. He saw the souls acting like mad dogs as they ripped each other's flesh apart. Instead of the sound of angel choirs, as in Heaven, St. John Bosco heard screams, shrieks, and curses against the saints.

As St. Bosco was taken to the lower levels of Hell, he saw some of his boys infested with vermin and worms. They were in Hell for many reasons, some for not being sorry for their sins, others for withholding sins in Confession, some for impurity and worldliness. Specifically, he was told that "transgressions of this commandment [the sixth commandment] caused the eternal ruin to many boys."[89] Before his dream ended, St. John Bosco was commanded to touch one of the outside walls of Hell. There were a thousand walls between the rim of Hell and the actual fires of Hell, yet the heat of the outside wall was so painful that it tore the skin off his palm, and he could not sleep for several nights following this nightmare.

Bl. Anne Catherine Emmerich

Living at the same time as St. John Bosco was the mystic Bl. Anne Catherine Emmerich (1774–1824). She was a German Augustinian nun, who received several visions of Jesus, Mary, and the saints. She was also a stigmatist—that is, someone who bore the wounds of Christ. In particular, she suffered the crown of thorns on her head. Following the closure of her convent by the government in 1812, she sought lodging with a poor widow and she spent her

---

[88] *Forty Dreams*, 154.
[89] *Forty Dreams*, 161.

days confined to bed. In her book, *The Dolorous Passion of Jesus Christ*, she recounts Jesus' entire life. She tells us that following His death, Jesus visited the center of Hell, which she vividly describes:

> The exterior of Hell was appalling and frightful; it was an immense, heavy-looking building, and the granite of which it was formed, although black, was of metallic brightness; and the dark and ponderous doors were secured with such terrible bolts that no one could behold them without trembling. Deep groans and cries of despair might be plainly distinguished even while the doors were tightly closed; but, oh, who can describe the dreadful yells and shrieks which burst upon the ear when the bolts were unfastened and the doors flung open; and, oh, who can depict the melancholy appearance of the inhabitants of this wretched place![90]

Bl. Anne Catherine points out that Jesus' "countenance was most severe"[91] during His visit to Hell. Unlike Heaven which was well-ordered, spacious, and beautiful, Hell was utter chaos, crowded, and painful. The exquisite flowers and fruit trees of Heaven were replaced by the "dismal dungeons, dark caverns, frightful deserts, [and] fetid swamps" of Hell.[92] Furthermore, "peace and happiness" pervade Heaven, while "anguish and despair" fill Hell.[93]

Those in Hell have one thought that consumes them: God's justice is giving them what they have chosen, and thus what they deserve.[94] Bl. Anne Catherine relates that Jesus spoke first to the soul of Judas in Hell. All of the demons were then compelled to

90 *Dolorous Passion*, 347.
91 *Dolorous Passion*, 347.
92 *Dolorous Passion*, 348
93 *Dolorous Passion*, 348.
94 *Dolorous Passion*, 348.

adore Jesus, which was a most humiliating experience, far worse than any torment. At the center of Hell was a "dark and horrible-looking abyss" where Lucifer was chained.[95] According to Bl. Anne Catherine, Satan was engulfed by "sulphureous black smoke"[96] to hide his appearance. She admits that there is much more to be said about Hell.

St. Faustina

In the twentieth century, the Polish nun St. Maria Faustina Kowalska (1905–1938) was instrumental in spreading devotion to Divine Mercy. Jesus gave her many messages. Often overlooked in these messages is her visit to Hell.

> Today, I was led by an Angel to the chasms of Hell. It is a place of great torture; how awesomely large and extensive it is! The kinds of tortures I saw: the first torture that constitutes Hell is the loss of God; the second is perpetual remorse of conscience; the third is that one's condition will never change; the fourth is the fire that will penetrate the soul without destroying it—a terrible suffering, since it is purely spiritual fire, lit by God's anger; the fifth torture is continual darkness and a terrible suffocating smell, and, despite the darkness, the devils and the souls of the damned see each other and all the evil, both of others and their own; the sixth torture is the constant company of Satan; the seventh torture is horrible despair, hatred of God, vile words, curses and blasphemies. These are the

---

[95] *Dolorous Passion*, 349.
[96] *Dolorous Passion*, 349.

tortures suffered by all the damned together, but that is not the end of the sufferings. There are special tortures destined for particular souls. These are the torments of the senses. Each soul undergoes terrible and indescribable sufferings, related to the manner in which it has sinned. There are caverns and pits of torture where one form of agony differs from another. I would have died at the very sight of these tortures if the omnipotence of God had not supported me. Let the sinner know that he will be tortured throughout all eternity, in those senses which he made use of to sin. I am writing this at the command of God, so that no soul may find an excuse by saying there is no Hell, or that nobody has ever been there, and so no one can say what it is like.[97]

God commanded St. Faustina to write down her terrifying visit to Hell, though she admitted that her words fell short of what she saw. At the same time, she mentioned something very profound: "But I noticed one thing: that most of the souls there are those who disbelieved that there is a Hell."[98] So shocking was her visit that St. Faustina said she could barely recover from her visit to Hell. As a result, she began to intensify her prayers for the conversion of sinners, asking for God's mercy to be upon them. St. Faustina even went onto say, "I would rather be in agony until the end of the world, amidst the greatest sufferings, than offend You by the least sin."[99]

---

[97] St. Maria Faustina Kowalska, *Diary: Divine Mercy in My Soul* (Stockbridge, MA: Marians of the Immaculate Conception, 2001), 296–297.
[98] *Diary*, 297.
[99] *Diary*, 297.

St. Faustina had another vision in which two of her religious sisters were about to enter Hell for committing mortal sins. Jesus told St. Faustina to let the superior know. She saw souls of religious who were in Hell for not observing silence (time protected in religious life for prayer and reflection). St. Faustina also was given a vision of two roads. One road was full of dancing and pleasures, and that road ended in Hell. Souls on that road were more numerous than she could count. The other road was full of suffering in this life, but that road ended in a beautiful garden.

Jesus told St. Faustina how much the devil hates every person, but especially her because she was rescuing many souls from his snares. The devil assaulted her throughout her life to stop the work of mercy. He once shook her bed and would often break objects in her room. He whispered doubts and lies to her, but she quickly banished them with prayer. St. Faustina noted the sheer ugliness of Satan, describing him as "more disgusting than all the torments of Hell."[100] Of all the torments the devil experienced, God's mercy is his greatest torment, according to St. Faustina. The devil does not want souls to believe that God is merciful and good, but only just.

The saints are prophets, but as with all prophets, many people in every generation still refuse to heed their voice. God has also sent His Mother at various times in Church history to warn us, to give the *final* warning. She is often called the "Mother of Mercy." Her prayers hold back her Son's justice, though He would much prefer to offer mercy.

[100] *Diary*, 230.

Questions for Reflection

❖ What stood out, struck you, or
moved you in this chapter?

❖ Which saintly vision inspired
you the most, and why?

❖ What would you do now if God
showed you your place in Hell?

❖ Have these revelations of Hell motivated you
to pray for others? If so, how specifically?

❖ How often do you think about the Four Last
Things: death, judgment, Hell, and Heaven? If you
do not meditate frequently on them, why not?

6

Marian Apparitions and Hell

———◇———

St. Thérèse of Lisieux's prayers for the conversion of Henri Pranzini echo those of another woman who prayed for the conversion of two criminals. Those criminals were flanking her dying Son. Although this notion is not mentioned by the Gospel writers, certainly the Blessed Mother's prayers at Calvary helped bring about the conversion of the good thief. She who had notified her Son of the wine running out at Cana now asks her Son for an even greater request: to sprinkle the new wine of His blood on the two sinners on either side of Him. Indeed, Jesus' blood filled the once lifeless soul of the good thief as he asked Jesus to remember him in Paradise. But the bad thief seemed to reject that grace. How many souls end up in Hell because no one warns them, let alone prays for them?

The Blessed Mother has been warning us about the reality of Hell for centuries. In Matthew's Gospel, we hear the parable of the wicked tenants (21:33–41). A householder builds a vineyard and lends it out to tenants. The householder sends various servants to collect his produce from the tenants, and the tenants kill them. At last, the householder sends his son, whom they also kill. That son was none other than Jesus. And now, when God sends His Mother to earth with a message, will people heed His Mother? To paraphrase the words of Jesus, "They will respect my Mother." Though we cannot kill Mary, we can kill in our hearts her message, which is ultimately her Son's message, by ignoring it or doubting it. We can also permanently harm our souls by choosing mortal sin without repenting. The Blessed Mother does whatever her Son tells her; that is, she appears only with her Son's permission and says what He wants her to say. Will we respect and heed Mary's message?

Private revelation does not add to or supersede public revelation (Sacred Scripture and Sacred Tradition), but it can deepen our understanding of them. Let us look at some approved Marian apparitions that shed further light on Hell and punishment. These apparitions are just a handful that the Catholic Church has declared as being authentic. Though Catholics are not required to believe these apparitions, the messages given in them continue to unfold in salvation history and are consistent with the teachings of Jesus and the saints. Therefore, these messages appear to be Our Lady's last call for conversion before the end times. And we would be wise to pay attention.

Our Lady of Fatima

In a small town in Portugal, the Blessed Mother appeared to three shepherd children—siblings St. Francisco Marto (age eight) and St. Jacinta Marto (age six) and their cousin Ven. Sr. Lucia dos Santos (age nine)—on six occasions from May to October 1917. Our Lady asked the three children to pray the Rosary and to offer sacrifices for the conversion of sinners. In her July 13, 1917, message, Our Lady showed the children a most disturbing vision of Hell. She reminded the visionaries that many souls were lost because no one would sacrifice for them. Sr. Lucia described the vision of Hell as follows:

> Our Lady showed us a great sea of fire which seemed to
> be under the earth. Plunged in this fire were demons and

souls in human form, like transparent burning embers, all blackened or burnished bronze, floating about in the conflagration, now raised into the air by the flames that issued from within themselves together with great clouds of smoke, now falling back on every side like sparks in a huge fire, without weight or equilibrium, and amid shrieks and groans of pain and despair, which horrified us and made us tremble with fear. The demons could be distinguished by their terrifying and repellent likeness to frightful and unknown animals, all black and transparent.[101]

After this terrifying vision, the Blessed Mother declared: "You have seen Hell, where the souls of poor sinners go. To save them, God wishes to establish in the world devotion to my Immaculate Heart. If what I say to you is done, many souls will be saved and there will be peace."[102] Sr. Lucia mentioned that the visionaries would have "died of fear and terror"[103] after seeing Hell, had Our Lady not shown them Heaven in the first apparition.

At the same time, the vision of Hell did not "traumatize"the young visionaries, according to Sr. Angela de Fatima Coelho, who

[101] Lucia de Jesus, *Fatima in Lucia's Own Words: Sr. Lucia's Memoirs*, trans. Dominican Nuns of Perpetual Rosary (Fatima: Postulation Centre, 1976), 104.

[102] *In Lucia's Own Words*, 104. Our Lady of Fatima went on to explain the secret of Fatima, which consisted of this vision of Hell, devotion to the Immaculate Heart of Mary (including by attending Mass and receiving Communion on the first Saturday of five consecutive months and making reparation for sinners), and the persecution of the Church and the Holy Father. Our Lady also asked for the consecration of Russia and predicted that another, greater war would take place if her message wasn't heeded.

[103] *In Lucia's Own Words*, 104.

served as the postulator for the cause for canonization of St. Francisco and St. Jacinta.[104] Rather, the vision inspired the children to help save more souls. The visionaries, especially St. Jacinta, realized that no penance was too great. They had no doubt that Hell was real. As Sr. Lucia declared, "What is certain is that Hell exists, and it is something about which Our Lady is greatly concerned. This is clear from her Message, in which She asks several times for prayers and sacrifices for the conversion of sinners."[105]

In that July apparition, Our Lady gave the children a prayer to be prayed after each decade of the Rosary: "O my Jesus, forgive us, save us from the fire of Hell. Lead all souls to Heaven, especially those who are most in need."[106] Our Lady was clear: "Save us from the fire of Hell." She did not say, "Save us from earthly suffering or from Purgatory." She clearly mentioned the fire of Hell.

A month after the vision of Hell, on August 13, Our Lady gave another urgent message: "Pray, pray very much, and make sacrifices for sinners; for many souls go to Hell, because there are none to sacrifice themselves and to pray for them."[107] The visionaries readily embraced Our Lady's summons to save sinners. For instance, they would give away their lunches to poor children whenever they saw them. Once St. Jacinta ate bitter food as a sacrifice. They also deprived themselves of water on a hot day.

---

[104] Sr. Angela de Fatima Coelho, *Inside the Light: Understanding the Message of Fatima* (Gastonia, NC: TAN Books, 2020), 102.

[105] Lucia de Jesus, *The Message of Fatima: How I See the Message in the Course of Time and in the Light of Events* (Fatima: Carmelo de Coimbra: Secretariado dos Pastorinhos, 2006), 50.

[106] *In Lucia's Own Words*, 162, 166. Today this prayer has been adapted in the United States. See appendix C.

[107] *In Lucia's Own Words*, 167.

Of all the Fatima visionaries, St. Jacinta was the most disturbed by Hell. She once grabbed Sr. Lucia and said this: "I'm going to Heaven, but you are staying here. If Our Lady lets you, tell everybody what Hell is like, so that they won't commit any more sins and not go to Hell."[108] According to Sr. Lucia, St. Jacinta would often ponder Hell and say the following: "Oh, Hell! Hell! How sorry I am for the souls who go to Hell! And the people down there, burning alive, like wood in the fire!"[109] But St. Jacinta did not stop there. She would then kneel and pray the prayer Our Lady taught her: "O my Jesus! Forgive us, save us from the fire of Hell. Lead all souls to heaven, especially those who are most in need!"[110]

Our Lady of Fatima told St. Jacinta that sins of impurity send the most souls to Hell. Keep in mind that this was back in the early twentieth century. Today, the sins of impurity are even more rampant, with the latest immodest fashions and accessibility to pornography. At Fatima, the angel of Portugal also appeared to the children and urged them to sacrifice for the conversion of sinners. He concluded with these words: "Above all, accept and bear with submission the suffering which the Lord will send you."[111]

On October 13, 1930, Fatima was officially approved by the bishop of Leiria, D. José Alves Correia da Silva.

Our Lady of Kibeho

In 1981, more than sixty years after her Fatima apparitions, Our Lady once again visited Earth. This time she appeared to

---

108 *In Lucia's Own Words*, 106.
109 *In Lucia's Own Words*, 105.
110 *In Lucia's Own Words*, 105.
111 *In Lucia's Own Words*, 62.

Alphonsine Mumureke (age seventeen), Nathalie Mukamazimpaka (age twenty), and Marie Claire Mukangango (age twenty-one) at their school in the tiny village of Kibeho, Rwanda. And as in Fatima, Our Lady predicted that bloodshed would ensue if people did not repent. Our Lady showed the visionaries the afterlife on separate occasions. Alphonsine described Hell as such: "The first place Mary took me was dark and very frightening. It was filled with shadows and groans of sadness and pain. She called it 'the Place of Despair,' where the road leading away from God's light ends."[112]

Our Lady took another visionary, Nathalie, to Heaven, Purgatory, and Hell. Nathalie described Hell in these words:

> The last place we visited was a land of twilight where the only illumination was an unpleasant shade of red that reminded me of congealed blood. The heat that rose from that world was stifling and dry—it brushed my face like a flame, and I feared that my skin would blister and crack. I couldn't look at the countless people who populated that unhappy place because their misery and anguish pained me so greatly. Mary didn't have to say the name of this place....
> I knew I was in Hell.[113]

This heat of Hell the visionary experienced is consistent with Jesus' words in the Gospel. This is because Our Lady's visions and messages never contradict the Gospel but only shed light on what her Son has already said and what is written throughout Scripture. Notice that the visionary says "countless people" inhabited Hell. Did not Our Lady of Fatima show the three children a similar

---

[112] Immaculée Ilibagiza, *Our Lady of Kibeho: Mary Speaks to the World from the Heart of Africa* (New York: Hay House, 2008), 135.
[113] Ilibagiza, *Our Lady of Kibeho*, 137.

vision? What can we conclude from these approved apparitions? There are, as Jesus said, "many" on the road to destruction and "few" on the narrow way to Heaven. Hell is far from being empty; Hell is overpopulated.

The visionaries also saw a river of blood and people killing each other, which predicted the future genocide in Rwanda. Our Lady was weeping as she showed these future events. This was not a vision of Hell but a vision of Hell on earth. Our Lady asked that people truly repent for hurting themselves and others. On March 27, 1982, Our Lady told Marie Claire, "The world is evil and rushes towards its ruin. It is about to fall in its abyss. The world is in rebellion against GOD. Many sins are being committed. There is no love and no peace. If you do not repent and convert your hearts, you will all fall into an abyss."[114] Sadly, the Rwandan genocide resulted in nearly one million deaths in the span of one hundred days in 1994. Rwandans suffered immensely, seeing family members chopped into pieces by their own countrymen with machetes right in front of their eyes.

Before the genocide took place, Our Lady of Kibeho gave the visionary Nathalie an important reminder regarding the centrality of suffering. Our Lady said, "No one goes to heaven without suffering. And as a child of Mary, you may never put down the cross you bear."[115] Suffering for the sake of suffering will not save us from Hell. But suffering united with Jesus and Mary for the sake of our souls and for the salvation of others can keep us on the narrow road to Heaven.

---

[114] Michael O'Neill, "Messages of Kibeho," The Miracle Hunter, https://miraclehunter.com/marian_apparitions/messages/kibeho _messages.html.

[115] Ilibagiza, *Our Lady of Kibeho*, 49.

As at Fatima, many people did not heed Our Lady of Kibeho's requests for prayer and repentance. Specifically, Our Lady of Kibeho asked people to pray the Rosary of the Seven Sorrows frequently, but especially on Tuesdays and Fridays. All of these warnings bring us back to the parable of the rich man and Lazarus, in which the rich man begged Abraham for some way to warn his relatives about Hell (see Luke 16:19–31). Sadly, Our Lady's messages continue to go ignored as souls continue to fall into Hell like snowflakes.

Bishop Augustin Misago of Gikongoro approved the Kibeho apparitions on June 29, 2001.

Our Lady of Champion

In 1859, less than two years after Our Lady appeared in Lourdes, France, she came to a small town in Wisconsin, today known as Champion. Our Lady appeared to Adele Brise (age twenty-eight), a Belgian immigrant who became a third order sister and founded the Sisters of St. Francis of Assisi. Although Our Lady did not show Hell to Sr. Adele, she gave her a serious warning:

I am the Queen of Heaven who prays for the conversion of sinners, and I wish you to do the same. You received Holy Communion this morning and that is well. But you must do more. Make a general confession and offer Communion for the conversion of sinners. If they do not convert and do penance, my Son will be obliged to punish them.[116]

---

[116] "Our Story," National Shrine of Our Lady of Champion, https://championshrine.org/our-story/. See also Patrick O'Hearn, *Go and Fear Nothing: The Story of Our Lady of Champion* (Huntington, IN: OSV Kids, 2023).

In 1871, the largest and deadliest fire in U.S. history broke out just sixty miles north of Champion, in Peshtigo, Wisconsin. The fire claimed 2,500 victims and burned more than 1.2 million acres. That night, as the fire surrounded them, Sr. Adele and her sisters, along with many families, prayed the Rosary and carried a statue of Mary in their chapel. Our Lady protected them as rain burst from the sky in the morning. Miraculously, the six acres where the Blessed Mother had appeared and where the chapel stood were left untouched. It was the only place not harmed by the fire for hundreds of miles.

The Peshtigo fire foreshadows the eternal fires awaiting unrepentant sinners in Hell. Punishment is a vehicle God can use to bring us back to Himself when we have strayed. Or in the words of Scripture: "The LORD reproves him whom he loves, as a father the son in whom he delights" (Prov. 3:12). And if we persist in sin, eternal punishment is a real possibility.

Approved by Bishop David Ricken of the Diocese of Green Bay on December 8, 2010, Our Lady of Champion remains the only approved Marian apparition in the United States.

Our Lady of Akita

On July 6, 1973, Our Lady appeared to Sr. Agnes Sasagawa (age forty-two) of the Order of the Handmaids of the Eucharist, at her convent in Akita, Japan. Our Lady did not come alone. Sr. Agnes's guardian angel also appeared to her. Sr. Agnes received three apparitions from July 6 to October 13, 1973. Like Sr. Adele, Sr. Agnes received stern messages about future punishments if mankind did not repent of its sinfulness. While Our Lady of Akita did not show Hell to Sr. Agnes, Our Lady's messages foreshadowed a future Hell on earth.

The Truth about Hell

On August 3, 1973, Our Lady said that the "Heavenly Father is preparing to inflict a great chastisement on all mankind. With My Son I have intervened so many times to appease the wrath of the Father."[117] Our Lady asked Sr. Agnes for prayer and penance to appease the Father's wrath. On October 13, 1973, fifty-six years to the day after the Miracle of Fatima took place—in which the sun literally spun toward the earth—Our Lady gave one of the most terrifying messages. She told Sr. Agnes the following:

> As I told you, if men do not repent and better themselves, the Father will inflict a terrible punishment on all humanity. It will be a punishment greater than the deluge, such as one will never have seen before. Fire will fall from the sky and will wipe out a great part of humanity, the good as well as the bad, sparing neither Priests nor faithful. The survivors will find themselves so desolate, that they will envy the dead. The only arms which remain for you will be the Rosary and the Sign left by My Son (the Eucharist). Each day recite the prayers of the Rosary. With the Rosary, pray for the Pope, the Bishops, and the Priests.[118]

In that same apparition, Our Lady said that the "work of the devil will infiltrate even into the Church in such a way that one will see Cardinals opposing Cardinals, Bishops against other Bishops."[119] Our Lady of Akita then mentioned how faithful priests will be persecuted while many in the Church will "accept compromises,"[120] and still many more priests and religious will

---

[117] Bob and Penny Lord, *The Many Faces of Mary: Book II: The Love Story Continues* (Morrilton, AR: Journeys of Faith, 2003), 238.

[118] *Many Faces*, 240–241.

[119] *Many Faces*, 241.

[120] *Many Faces*, 241.

abandon their vocations. She also stated that the demon will target consecrated souls. Our Lady was troubled by so much sin, especially the betrayal by God's chosen ones. She declared, "The thought of the loss of so many souls is the cause of My sadness. If sins increase in number and gravity, there will no longer be pardon for them."[121] Many consecrated sons and daughters have rejected God's will, thus piercing Jesus' and Mary's hearts all over again.

Hell could be likened to a perpetual cloister of sorrow where unfaithful souls, especially religious, send up cries to the devil for all eternity, rather than praise God. Since these consecrated souls served Satan in their earthly lives, they will continue serving him forever. Satan will be their abbot and their slave master. What incomprehensible sadness to forfeit eternal happiness for a few fleeting pleasures and for accepting compromises rather than obeying and loving Jesus and His Church!

Our Lady's final words to Sr. Agnes show us that not all is lost, that future destruction and even Hell itself can be averted by prayer: "Pray very much the prayers of the Rosary. I alone am able to save you from the calamities which approach. Those who place their confidence in Me will be saved."[122] Another miraculous phenomenon took place in connection with these apparitions: the statue of Mary in the convent chapel where Mary appeared wept 101 times over a span of six years.

On April 22, 1984, Bishop John Shojiro Ito of Niigata approved the Akita apparitions.

---

[121] *Many Faces*, 241.

[122] *Many Faces*, 241. We are saved only through the Passion and Death of Jesus. When Our Lady promises to save us, it is always through Jesus.

Throughout history, the Blessed Mother has warned us of Hell, calling us to pray and sacrifice for the conversion of sinners. And she continues to weep as the world is becoming more and more depraved and as people lose the sense of sin. Hence, Our Lady's messages are becoming stronger and stronger as she and her Son continue to hold back the Father's wrath. In these dark times when the Father's patience "appears" to be running out and Satan's tentacles are grasping countless souls, we must call upon Our Lady more than ever. After all, Our Lady is the new Ark of the Covenant and likened to Noah's ark. From her Ark of Heaven, she throws each of us a lifeline as the floodwaters of our fallen world seek to engulf us. And that lifeline is none other than her Holy Rosary. Allow her to draw you to know Jesus in this holy prayer, and she will reel you into her Ark.

As the apostles feared being drowned on the Sea of Galilee during a rough storm and St. Peter cried out to Our Lord, let us invoke Mary, the Ark, and cry out: "Save us, O Mother, for we are perishing" (see Matt. 8:25). Save us, Jesus and Mary, from the fires of Hell. Or, best put by St. Alphonsus Ligouri: "If, then, we should be saved, let us recommend ourselves to Mary, that she may intercede for us, because her prayers are always heard. O Mother of mercy! have pity on me. Thou art styled the advocate of sinners; assist me, therefore, a sinner placing my confidence in thee."[123]

---

[123] St. Alphonsus Liguori, *The Way of Salvation and of Perfection* (New York: Benziger Brothers, 1886), 39.

Questions for Reflection

❖ What stood out, struck you, or
moved you in this chapter?

❖ Which Marian apparition inspired you
the most, and why? What are some ways
you show your love to the Blessed Mother
and her Son? Do you pray the Rosary and
the Rosary of the Seven Sorrows?

❖ Do you have a close relationship with
the Blessed Mother? If not, why not? If you
don't, what can you specifically commit
to, on a daily basis, to change that?

Conclusion

I (Dan) recently found myself in an ambulance. My pain was extreme, and I was in a neck brace, but the spiritual needs of the souls caring for me quickly became evident. One of the emergency medical technicians (EMTs) revealed that he was no longer going to Mass.

"How often do you see people die?" I asked him.

He replied, "Every day."

I asked, "How, then, are you not going to Mass and failing to be ready for your judgment, knowing that we can all die at any moment?"

He began his reply, "I am a good person."

I responded, "I have no doubt you are a good person, but being good doesn't solve the problem of sin. That is why Jesus came to give His life for our sins, to reconcile us to God. This is why we have the Church, the sacraments, and the priesthood." At the end of our conversation, he promised to return to Mass.

I don't know if he did return, but his perspective is common among Catholics, both those who attend Mass and those who do not. Many of us are truly "good" on a human level. We don't kick puppies, we are nice, we use our turn signals, we give our change to the bell ringers at Christmastime, and sometimes we even help out in our parishes. Even so, we fail to understand that "good" acts, in and of themselves, have no bearing on our standing before

God. Said another way, these "good" acts, when disconnected from a relationship with God, will not save us from Hell.

Why is this the case? Consider the claims of Jesus. Why did Jesus—God—become incarnate and suffer brutal torture, ridicule, and crucifixion if all we need to do to know and follow God is to be good? Why did God become man and die this kind of tragic death? He came because He loves us and wanted us to know and understand Him—to follow Him—to become His friend. He came and died in order to pay the price for our sins so that we could be reconciled to God, to enter into a relationship with Him, walk with Him, know Him, know peace, and live in His friendship in this life and in the next—Heaven.

A helpful question we were taught to ask during an evangelistic outreach is this: "When you get to the gates of Heaven and God asks, 'Why should I let you in?,' how will you answer?" The instinctive answer to this question reveals a great deal about how we think about our salvation. In fact, it would be good for you, the reader, to take a moment to answer this question in your head. How would you answer this question? Envision yourself standing before God. What is your answer? Take a moment and write your response out in a sentence or two.

Did your answer begin with how good you are and what you have done or not done? Or does your answer begin with what Jesus has done on your behalf? The latter answer is one that most likely will yield your desired end—Heaven. I pray that the former is far less likely to come from a reader who has truly paid attention to the wisdom of this book. If your answer began with your goodness or things you have done, even to or for God, we urge you to reread this book and to spend time daily reading and meditating on the Gospels so that you can get a better handle on what it means to be a disciple of Jesus. The best answer always begins with one all-important word: *Jesus*. It sounds something like this: "Jesus is the only reason You should let me in. Yes, I have tried to be good. Yes, I have done my best to honor You, but ultimately nothing matters without His sacrifice on my behalf, for which I am grateful. I don't deserve to be here, but I would be grateful if, because of what Jesus has done on my behalf, You would let me in." This kind of prayer is irresistible to God and one that won't be denied.

If you are feeling a bit unsure, don't worry. In the following appendix, "What Next?," we have provided all you need in order to understand what it means to know and follow Jesus and to live it.

Appendix A

What Next?

Has this book scared the Hell out of you? Well, that is not a bad thing. The challenge is that sin and selfishness, fueled by concupiscence, is a kind of Hell-bound gravity or force pulling us the wrong way. The good news is that God's remedy is stronger; His grace is far more powerful and can easily win the tug of war within us so that we find and remain on the narrow way to Heaven.

Some important questions to ask yourself are these: "What specific steps can I take today in light of what has been revealed to me in this book? How can I put this wisdom to work in my life so that I can live and walk in the peace that comes to those who follow Jesus closely?

What follows are several recommendations for the soul who is truly motivated to turn away from Hell and turn toward God and His mercy.

1. *Begin reading and praying through the Gospels every day.* Dan Burke's book *Into the Deep: Finding Peace through Prayer* was written to guide serious pilgrims on this path to knowing and following Jesus. The reader can also find free film series on mental prayer at SpiritualDirection.com/pray.

2. *Begin frequenting the sacraments of the Eucharist and Penance more often.* The best practice for the Sacrament of Penance is to go at least once a month. Souls truly intent on traversing the hard terrain on the narrow way should receive the Eucharist as often as

possible; strive for more than just the Sunday obligation to attend Mass, as your circumstances and state of life allow.

3. *Begin making a brief daily examen*, or examination of conscience, to assess your movements toward or away from God during the day. Consider tracking in a journal your progress and goals for growth in virtue. This will be a valuable tool to discuss with your spiritual director and can assist you in preparing your plan of life and in making solid confessions.

4. *Begin praying the Rosary daily.* Don't, however, treat the Rosary as if praying it is a magic get-out-of-Hell incantation. Praying the Rosary is meant to allow Mary to lead you in contemplation to Jesus, not to be a quick, mindless buzzing through beads that St. Teresa of Avila says is not really praying at all. If you already pray the Rosary and would like to know a deeper path in this devotion, read Dan's book *The Contemplative Rosary*.

5. *Study the wisdom of the Paradigm of Ascent* below and take the free course on this topic on ApostoliViae.org. These foundational practices and formation will provide you with a rich experience and spiritual growth that will allow you to understand what it means to truly follow Jesus and to find peace that you are heading to Heaven and not to Hell.

The Paradigm of Ascent as a Pathway Forward

To help you better understand the dynamics of this journey, we provide below a brief summary of what we call the Paradigm of Ascent.™ [124] This framework represents the foundational practices

---

[124] Note that this trademark is to ensure its proper use. It is a very simple but powerful model that can easily be trivialized by those who use it without sufficient formation behind each of its components.

of every saint of the past and of every holy person alive today. The truths revealed in the paradigm are foundational in that, if they are not all present in some substantive way in your life, a deeper understanding of the interior life will remain beyond your grasp and you will likely lose your way on the narrow path to Heaven. This is a bad thing only if you fail to take the next steps to remedy whatever deficiency you uncover.

The first foundational truth is that you must have in your heart an authentic yes to God to begin your journey to Him. It is not enough merely to know about God or even to practice your Faith: you must know God intimately. This is the path of the mystics, but it is also the path every soul can know and must embrace to get to Heaven. This path is often obscure to most Catholics because it is not common for someone already in the Church to hear a pronounced or dramatic call to conversion. This call to conversion and even the warnings of Hell, however, were offered frequently by Jesus to those who were among His closest followers. Though you have been baptized and confirmed, you still must constantly recognize your need for God and for the conversion of life that draws you ever closer to Him.

The second foundational element is the most important support for your yes of the heart, and it consists of the Sacraments of the Eucharist and regular Confession. You should participate in the Holy Sacrifice of the Mass not only on Sundays (because it is a mortal sin to miss Mass on Sunday without good reason) but as frequently as possible, because the Eucharist is the most powerful sustenance of your faith. The Sacrament of Penance and Reconciliation (Confession) is also necessary to support your yes. Too often, Catholics underestimate the power of this sacrament. You might think of it merely as a remedy for sin, which it is, but it is also a great grace to strengthen you against falling into sin again. Said another way, the Sacrament of Penance both provides forgiveness of sins *and* strengthens you in your efforts to fight sin. It is also the most significant weapon in the Church's arsenal against Satan in spiritual warfare. Regardless, if you are not reconciled to God and not living in a state of grace, you are cut off from the life of grace and will not be able to discern properly the difference between the inspirations and influence of God and the temptations and false lies of the devil. If you are not in a state of grace, you have fundamentally said no to God and His plan for your life and yes to the devil and are on the road to Hell.

Because of the rampant poor catechesis of our time, we must be absolutely clear on this point. Living in a state of grace means that you are living without having unconfessed mortal sins, and you are following the teachings of the Church in every aspect of your life. The *Catechism of the Catholic Church* is very clear on these matters and should be studied by every serious Catholic. The diagram below reveals the beginning elements of your foundation in the paradigm to ascend to greater holiness and their relationship with one another.

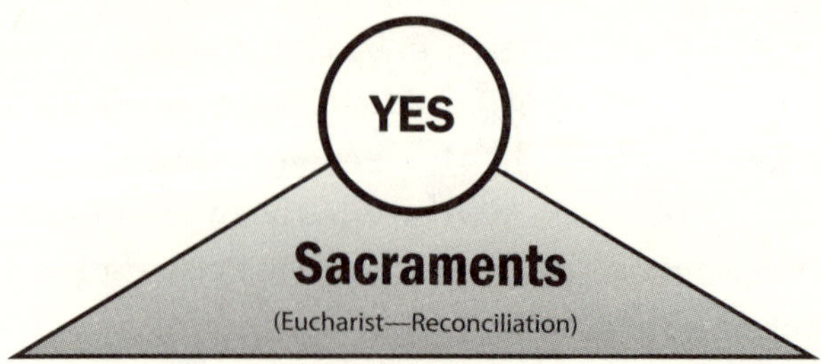

The third foundational element to authentic discipleship is daily prayer. The most powerful daily prayers are mental prayer and the Rosary. Sts. Teresa of Avila and Alphonsus Liguori, both Doctors of the Church, consider daily mental prayer to be necessary for salvation because of the impact on the soul of those who daily draw near to their Savior in dedicated intimacy. A sound and very practical understanding of the practice of daily mental prayer can be found in Dan's book *Into the Deep*. The Rosary, as revealed by our Blessed Mother, is necessary both for your salvation and that of the world. Together, these two daily practices provide protection as a kind of shield and nurture your yes, which allows you to move forward in faith.[125] With these daily practices in place, our diagram now looks like this and begs for a final aspect necessary for balance.

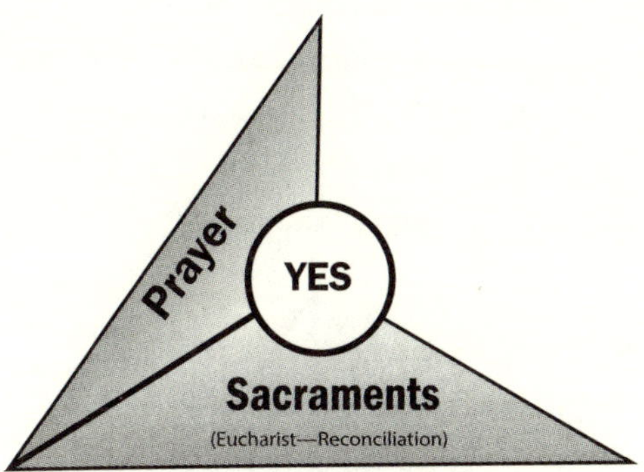

The fourth foundational element to your progress on the narrow way is *ascesis*. This ancient Greek word simply means "exercise." In our usage, that exercise is to exert conscious daily and deliberate

---

[125] Whether you have yet to take up the practice of the Rosary or are a long-time practitioner and need to go deeper or break the pattern of rote familiarity, you will find helpful *The Contemplative Rosary*, by Dan Burke and Connie Rossini.

effort to move away from sin and selfishness and toward self-giving to God and your neighbor. It is the practical result of what Jesus meant when He said, "If any man would come after me, let him deny himself and take up his cross and follow me" (Matt. 16:24). Ascesis is purposeful self-denial for the sake of self-giving—saying no to the draws of your lower nature in order to say yes to giving yourself completely to God and to those whom He has placed in your care. Ascesis is simply what it means to truly follow Jesus. The funny thing is that if you pursue the sacraments and prayer the way the saints did, your practice of ascesis is already well underway!

This final element completes what we like to call a "saint-making machine." These basic elements are in place in the life of every saint and everyone who makes progress in the spiritual life toward God and peace and away from sin and the sorrows of sin. This Paradigm of Ascent™ is also the necessary basis for beginning to distinguish between the voice and influence of God and the voice and influence of the enemy of your soul.

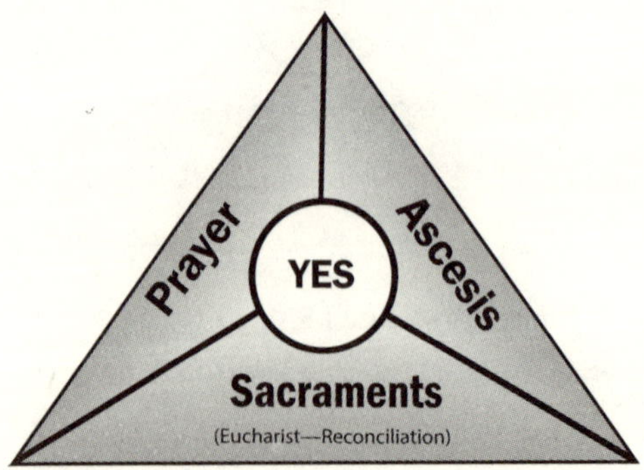

As you begin to implement these practices, you will, by God's grace and provision, lay a foundation that is, in and of itself, the most powerful healing and liberating force you can know. You will begin living by what is known in Catholic Tradition as a rule of life, or what we call in our community of Apostoli Viae, a "plan of love." A plan of love is simply a purposeful way to live and love God and those He has placed in our care. A good plan always has concrete commitments that you make to God and your loved ones on a daily, weekly, or monthly basis. A simple plan of love might look something like this:

* Daily mental prayer: wake up at 6:00 a.m. and pray for ten minutes, focusing on that day's Gospel reading for Mass.
* Daily Rosary: pray one decade on the way to work.
* Attend Mass every Sunday without fail.
* Go to Confession every other week.

The final step in your foundation is what is known as the examen. You might have heard the following phrase in business "What gets measured gets done." The same principle applies in the life of the soul who truly desires to give itself to God and to know the peace and joy He has for it. It is common to hear folks shy away from the examen because they have been taught a predominantly negative approach that is solely focused on where they have failed or what they have done wrong. This is not the approach we recommend. Instead, we encourage practicing the examen in a way that is focused on God's redemptive power and mercy, not on your weaknesses and failures. As St. Paul recalled, "He said to me, 'My grace is sufficient for you, for my power is made perfect in weakness.' … For when I am weak, then I am strong" (2 Cor. 12:9–10).

The approach we recommend looks something like this: Every night before going to bed, take five minutes to review your day. Ask the Lord and the Blessed Mother to reveal what you need to know. Then step into your "mental helicopter," fly up about twenty feet, and then fly back to when you got out of bed in the morning. Then slowly fly over your day, from morning to evening, asking two simple questions:

1. *What have I been able to do, by the grace of God, that honors Him and others?* When you discover these things, express praise and thanksgiving to God. This can be as simple as "Thank You, Lord, for the ability to pray according to my plan of love when I didn't feel like doing so."

2. *How have I failed to love and honor God and others?* When you discover these things, continue to pray in thanksgiving, something like this: "Thank You, Lord, for revealing my sin to me so that I can be forgiven and strengthened to overcome this sin in the future. Thank You for Your promise and provision of forgiveness and strength against sin and temptation."

Now, this may seem very simple—and it is. Don't be fooled, however. This powerful practice is no less important than a compass is to someone seeking to find his way through the wilderness. It keeps you awake to your progress on the narrow way to Heaven, and it helps ensure that you stay on the path. It also perfects your trust in God and deepens your understanding of yourself as a beloved child, wholly dependent on His help and mercy for every good in your life.

Appendix B

Resources for Continued Spiritual Growth

If you are ready to engage more intensely in the battle for peace and strength in the storm and deepen your relationship with the God who longs for you, go to ApostoliViae.org and create a free profile. Once you complete that process, go to the Courses page to find a series of free mini courses on overcoming habitual sin, discernment of spirits, mental prayer, the examen, and much more. As well, you will gain access to a printable summary guide for both the examen and the rules of discernment that will reinforce what you have read in this book and help you to learn and apply the powerful life-changing wisdom of the Church.

Here are additional recommended resources to help you on your journey.

Marian Devotion

The Contemplative Rosary: With St. John Paul II and St. Teresa of Avila by Dan Burke and Connie Rossini is a sure guide to praying the Rosary like a saint (SophiaInstitute.com).

Fatima in Lucia's Own Words by Sr. Lucia de Jesus is one of the best books written on Fatima, especially since it comes straight from Sr. Lucia.

Our Lady of Sorrows: Devotion to Mary's Seven Sorrows for Children by Patrick O'Hearn is a children's book with meditations and prayers to console Mary in her Seven Sorrows; the book includes four original prayers by Fr. Chad Ripperger (SophiaInstitute.com).

Prayer

Into the Deep: Finding Peace through Prayer by Dan Burke is the simplest, most straightforward book in print on how to begin or deepen your prayer life (SpiritualDirection.com/shop).

Raising Saints

Parents of the Saints: The Hidden Heroes Behind Our Favorite Saints by Patrick O'Hearn highlights the seven hallmarks of godly parents through the lives of fifty holy couples (TanBooks.com).

Spiritual Warfare

Spiritual Warfare and the Discernment of Spirits by Dan Burke gives a foundational understanding of the battleground of the mind, how the enemy works in this area, and how Scripture and the wisdom of St. Ignatius of Loyola can help you fight back against the world, the flesh, and the devil — and win (SpiritualDirection .com/shop).

Surrender

Finding Peace in the Storm by Dan Burke unpacks St. Alphonsus Liguori's classic work *Uniformity with God's Will* (SpiritualDirection.com/shop).

Daily Spiritual Sustenance

SpiritualDirection.com is meant to help you to grow spiritually by providing thousands of articles, videos, and other powerful materials rooted in the Magisterium and the faithful mystical tradition of the Church. Be sure to sign up for the e-mail digest, which will provide you with new insights on the journey every week.

Targeted Formation in the Spiritual Life and Spiritual Theology

The Avila Institute for Spiritual Formation (Avila-Institute.org) provides spiritual formation to laity, priests, and religious worldwide through live online classes. There are studies at a level for busy people as well as graduate studies for those who have the time and the inclination.

Faithful Catholic Community

The mission of the worldwide Catholic community of Apostoli Viae is to:

* *Live the Way*: to understand, wholeheartedly embrace, and joyfully live the contemplative life.
* *Light the Way*: to joyfully witness to, invite, reveal, and teach the contemplative path to all who thirst.
* *Lead the Way*: to generously, personally, and individually serve, form, and guide pilgrims on the path to union with God and love of neighbor.

If this sounds compelling to you, learn more at ApostoliViae.org.

Appendix C

Prayers for Spiritual Growth

Fatima Prayers

O my Jesus, forgive us our sins, save us from the fires of Hell. Lead all souls to Heaven, especially those most in need of Thy mercy.

Most Holy Trinity, Father, Son, and Holy Spirit, I offer You the most precious Body, Blood, Soul, and Divinity of Jesus Christ, present in all the tabernacles of the world, in reparation for the outrages, sacrileges, and indifference with which He Himself is offended. And, through the infinite merits of His most Sacred Heart, and the Immaculate Heart of Mary, I beg of You the conversion of poor sinners.

Prayer of Self-Offering[126]

Most Sacred Heart of Jesus, truly present in Holy Eucharist, I consecrate my body and soul to be entirely one with Your Heart, being sacrificed at every instant on all the altars of the world and giving praise to the Father, pleading for the coming of His Kingdom.

Please receive this humble offering of myself. Use me as You will for the glory of the Father and the salvation of souls.

---

[126] This prayer was prayed by Sr. Agnes's community. Our Lady asked Sr. Agnes to insert the word "truly" before "present."

Most holy Mother of God, never let me be separated from Your Divine Son. Please defend and protect me as your special child. Amen.

Prayer to the Most Holy Mary[127]

by St. Alphonsus Liguori

O Mary, thou dost so much desire to see this thy Son Jesus loved; if thou lovest me, this is the grace I ask of thee, and which thou must procure for me; obtain for me a great love for Jesus Christ, and not to love any other than Him. Thou obtainest from Him all that thou dost wish; listen to me, then, pray for me and comfort me; bind me in such a manner to Jesus, that I shall no longer be able to leave off loving Him. Obtain for me also a great love toward thee, who art of all creatures the most loving, the most lovely, and the most loved by God. I rely greatly on thy compassion, and I love thee, my Lady; but I love thee only a little: ask thy God to give me a greater love; for to love thee is a grace which God grants only to those whom thou dost wish to be saved.

Live, Jesus our love; live, Mary our hope!

[127] St. Alphonsus Liguori, *The Holy Mass* (New York: Benziger Brothers, 1889), 409.

Quotations on Hell

Our most important affair is that of our eternal salvation; upon it depends our happiness or misery for ever. This affair will come to an end in eternity, and will decide whether we shall be saved or lost forever; whether we shall have acquired an eternity of delights, or an eternity of torments; whether we shall live forever happy, or forever miserable. (St. Alphonsus Liguori)[128]

____

He who prays not is certain to be damned. All the saints were saved, and came to be saints by praying; all the accursed souls in Hell were lost through neglect of prayer; if they had prayed, it is certain that they would not have been lost. And this will be one of the greatest occasions of their anguish in Hell, the thought that they might have saved themselves so easily; that they had only to beg God to help them, but that now the time is past when this could avail them. (St. Alphonsus Liguori)[129]

____

The gate of Heaven is narrow: to enter it we must labour, and must do violence to ourselves. And we ought to be persuaded that what we can do today, we shall not be always able to do hereafter. The

[128] *Way of Salvation*, 15.
[129] *Way of Salvation*, 430.

delay of conversion sends many Christians to Hell. (St. Alphonsus Liguori)[130]

When a soul leaves off prayer, it is as if she cast herself into Hell without any need of the devils. (St. Teresa of Avila)[131]

In the long run, the answer to all those who object to the doctrine of hell, is itself a question: "What are you asking God to do?" To wipe out their past sins, and at all costs, to give them a fresh start, smoothing over every difficulty and offering every miraculous help? But He has done so, on Calvary. To forgive them? They will not be forgiven. To leave them alone? Alas, I am afraid that is what He does. (C. S. Lewis)[132]

Some people, even the most devout, refuse to speak to children about Hell, in case it would frighten them. Yet God did not hesitate to show Hell to three children, one of whom was only six years old, knowing well that they would be horrified to the point of, I would almost say, withering away with fear. (Sr. Lucia dos Santos)[133]

Depart, accursed fathers and mothers! Depart into the Hell where the wrath of God awaits you, you and the good deeds you have

---

[130] *Sermons of St. Alphonsus*, 399.

[131] St. Alphonsus Liguori, *The Holy Eucharist* (New York: Benziger Brothers, 1887), 344.

[132] *The Problem of Pain* (New York: Macmillan, 1947), 116.

[133] *In Lucia's own words*, 105.

done, while all the time you have let your children run wild. Depart into Hell; they will not be long in joining you there. (St. John Vianney)[134]

———————————

God was so displeased with pride that He did not spare to drive down into Hell the noble, high, excellent angels of heaven for the sake of their pride. So who in this wretched world could have a status so high that he would not have serious cause to tremble and quake in every joint of his body as soon as he feels a high, proud thought enter his heart? (St. Thomas More)[135]

———————————

He who has had the misfortune of having committed a mortal sin must go to confession immediately; for he may die any moment, and be damned. You may say: "I will go to confession at Easter or Christmas." And how do you know that you will not die suddenly in the meantime? "I hope in God that I shall not!" But should it happen, what must become of you? How many have kept saying, "Hereafter, hereafter," and are now in Hell: because death came upon them, and they were not able to make their confession. (St. Alphonsus Liguori)[136]

———————————

How many do you think will be saved out of our city [of Antioch]? Not out of so many thousands will a hundred be found! And it is doubtful that there will even be this number. How much

---

[134] Quoted in Paul Thigpen, *A Dictionary of Quotes from the Saints* (Charlotte, NC: TAN Books, 2001), 101.
[135] Quoted in Thigpen, *Dictionary of Quotes*, 223.
[136] *Preaching*, 527.

wickedness there is among the young! How much sloth among the old! No-one has zeal: we are like a pile of straw! (St. John Chrysostom)[137]

The Church is a barn in which there is much chaff but only a few grains of wheat. There are more wicked than good; there are more to be damned than saved. (St. Augustine)[138]

Broad is the way to the pleasures of the world, and there is no work involved in finding it, for it offers itself willingly. All find the way [to salvation] to be narrow, and many of those who find it do not enter into it. There are many who, captured by the pleasures of the world, turn themselves away in the middle of the journey of truth. (St. Bede the Venerable)[139]

The damned shall ask the devils what is the hour of the night. "Watchmen, what of the night?" — Isa. xxi. 11. When shall it end? When shall these trumpets, these shrieks, this stench, these flames, these torments cease? Their answer is, *Never, never.* And how long shall they last? *Forever, forever.* Ah Lord, give light to so many blind Christians, who, when entreated not to damn themselves, say: "If I go to Hell, I must have patience." O God! they have not patience to bear the least cold, to remain in an overheated room, or to submit to a buffet on the cheek. And how can they have patience to

---

[137] Homily 40, to the people, cited in Cornelius a Lapide, *Commentary on Matthew* 14:13–14.

[138] St. Augustine, *Contra Cresconium*, cited in Cornelius a Lapide, *Commentary on Matthew* 14:13–14.

[139] *Exposition of the Gospel according to Matthew.*

remain in a sea of fire, trampled by the devils, and abandoned by God and by all, for all eternity? (St. Alphonsus Liguori)[140]

Do you really believe that some of them would reform if you were to warn them? Then and there your warning might impress them, but soon they will forget it, saying: "It was just a dream," and they will do worse than before. Others, realizing they have been unmasked, will receive the Sacraments, but this will be neither spontaneous nor meritorious; others will go to Confession because of a momentary fear of Hell, but will be attached to sin. (guide speaking to St. John Bosco)[141]

For which are more greatly to be feared, I ask you? Should we fear most greatly those tribulations which are here today and gone tomorrow, those fires which burn today and by tomorrow will be extinguished, those pains which spring up for a brief hour and within the same hour have passed? Or should we not rather fear much more tribulations which *never* end, the fire which shall never be extinguished, and the pains which will continue without relief for endless ages? (St. Sebastian)[142]

We are compelled to make known that he who perseveres in devotion to Mary and to the Rosary will not be damned; for Mary

---

[140] *Preparation for Death, or, Considerations on the Eternal Maxims* (Boston: Thomas Sweeney, 1854), 267.

[141] *Forty Dreams*, 154–155.

[142] Quoted in St. Ambrose of Milan, *A Tale of Death and Glory: The Acts of St. Sebastian and His Companions*, trans. Fr. Robert Nixon, O.S.B. (Gastonia, NC: TAN Books, 2022), 26.

will secure for him eternal salvation. (demons speaking through a possessed heretic)[143]

If I saw the gates of Hell open and I stood on the brink of the abyss, I would not despair, I would not lose hope of mercy, because I would trust in You, my God. (St. Gemma Galgani)[144]

When the Devil tempts you, remember Hell; the thought of Hell will preserve you from that land of misery. I say, remember Hell, and have recourse to Jesus Christ and to most holy Mary, and they will deliver you from sin, which is the gate of Hell. (St. Alphonsus Liguori)[145]

I have been down there with those miserable [souls], and God let me feel the pain that the damned suffer. (St. Padre Pio)[146]

[143] *Preaching*, 133.

[144] Quoted in Thigpen, *Dictionary of Quotes*, 70.

[145] *Sermons of St. Alphonsus*, 83.

[146] Padre Pio said this to Cleonice Morcaldi, and she wrote about it in her published memoir, *La mia vita vecino a Padre Pio* (Rome: Dehoniane, 1997), 181

Bibliography

Akin, Jimmy. "Anathema." *Catholic Answers*, April 1, 2000. https://www.catholic.com/magazine/print-edition/anathema.

Ambrose of Milan, St. *A Tale of Death and Glory: The Acts of St. Sebastian and His Companions*. Translated by Fr. Robert Nixon, O.S.B. Gastonia, NC: TAN Books, 2022.

Anselm of Canterbury, St. *The Glories of Heaven: The Supernatural Gifts That Await Body and Soul in Paradise*. Translated by Fr. Robert Nixon, O.S.B. Gastonia, NC: TAN Books, 2022.

Aquinas, St. Thomas. *Catena Aurea*. Vol. 1. Translated by William Whiston. London: J. G. F. and J. Rivington, 1842.

———. *The Summa Theologiae of St. Thomas Aquinas*. 2nd rev. ed. Translated by the Fathers of the English Dominican Province. 1920. New Advent. https://www.newadvent.org/summa/.

Augustine, St. *The City of God*, 2 vols. Translated by Marcus Dods. New York: Hafner Publishing , 1948.

———. *Confessions of St. Augustine*. Boston: E. P. Peabody, 1842.

Bede the Venerable, St. "Hymnus de Die Judicii." Translated by Fr. Robert Nixon, O.S.B.

Benedict XVI, Pope. Encyclical letter *Spe Salvi*. November 30, 2007.

Bosco, St. John. *Forty Dreams of St. John Bosco, the Apostle of Youth: From the Biographical Memoirs of St. John Bosco.* Charlotte, NC: TAN Books, 2014.

Burke, Dan. *Finding Peace in the Storm: Reflections on St. Alphonsus Liguori's* Uniformity with God's Will. Manchester, NH: Sophia Institute Press, 2023.

Catherine of Siena, St. *The Dialogue of St. Catherine of Siena: A Conversation with God on Living Your Spiritual Life to the Fullest.* Charlotte, NC: TAN Books, 2010.

Coelho, Sr. Angela de Fatima. *Inside the Light: Understanding the Message of Fatima.* Gastonia, NC: TAN Books, 2020.

"Commentary on the Gospel: The Wedding Garment." Opus Dei. https://opusdei.org/en-ph/gospel/commentary-on-the-gospel -the-wedding-garment/#_ftn3.

de Jesus, Lucia. *Fatima in Lucia's Own Words: Sr. Lucia's Memoirs.* Translated by Dominican Nuns of Perpetual Rosary. Fatima: Postulation Centre, 1976.

———. *The Message of Fatima: How I See the Message in the Course of Time and in the Light of Events.* Fatima: Carmelo de Coimbra: Secretariado dos Pastorinhos, 2006.

Emmerich, Bl. Anne Catherine. *The Dolorous Passion of Our Lord Jesus Christ.* Charlotte, NC: TAN Books, 2012.

Fradd, Matt. "Becoming Saints." *Catholic Answers,* February 25, 2013. https://www.catholic.com/magazine/online-edition /becoming-saints.

Frances of Rome, St. *The Visions of Saint Frances of Rome: Hell, Purgatory, and Heaven Revealed.* Translated by Fr. Robert Nixon, O.S.B. Gastonia, NC: TAN Books, 2023.

Gignac, Joseph. "Anathema." *The Catholic Encyclopedia.* Vol. 1. New York: Robert Appleton, 1907. New Advent. https://www .newadvent.org/cathen/01455e.htm.

Grondin, Fr. Charles. "Did Sheol Become Gehenna after the Resurrection?" Catholic Answers. https://www.catholic.com/qa/did-sheol-become-gehenna-after-the-resurrection.

Hontheim, Joseph. "Hell." *The Catholic Encyclopedia*. Vol. 7. New York: Robert Appleton, 1910. https://www.newadvent.org/cathen/07207a.htm.

"How Many People Die Each Day in 2024?" World Population Review. https://worldpopulationreview.com/countries/deaths-per-day.

Horn, Trent. "Is the Road to Hell Paved with the Skulls of Priests?" *Catholic Answers*, September 5, 2018. https://www.catholic.com/magazine/online-edition/is-the-road-to-Hell-paved-with-the-skulls-of-priests.

Ilibagiza, Immaculée. *Our Lady of Kibeho: Mary Speaks to the World from the Heart of Africa*. New York: Hay House, 2008.

John of the Cross, St. *The Collected Works of St. John of the Cross*. Translated by Kieran Kavanaugh, O.C.D., and Otilio Rodriguez, O.C.D. Washington, D.C.: ICS Publications, 1973.

John Paul II, Pope St. General Audience. July 28, 1999.

Kowalska, St. Maria Faustina. *Diary: Divine Mercy in My Soul*. Stockbridge, MA: Marians of the Immaculate Conception, 2001.

Lewis, C.S. *The Problem of Pain*. New York: Macmillan, 1947.

Ligouri, St. Alphonsus. *The Holy Eucharist*. New York: Benziger Brothers, 1887.

———. *The Holy Mass*. New York: Benziger Brothers, 1889.

———. *Preaching*. New York: Benziger Brothers, 1890.

———. *Preparation for Death, or, Considerations on the Eternal Maxims*. Boston: Thomas Sweeney, 1854.

———. *The Sermons of St. Alphonsus Liguori for All the Sundays of the Year*. Charlotte, NC: TAN Books, 2012.

———. *Uniformity with God's Will*. Translated by Thomas W. Tobin, C.SS.R. Charlotte, NC: TAN Books, 2013.

———. *The Way of Salvation and of Perfection*. New York: Benziger Brothers, 1886.

Lord, Bob and Penny. *The Many Faces of Mary: Book II: The Love Story Continues*. Morrilton, AR: Journeys of Faith, 2003.

Mannion, Msgr. M. Francis. "What Does It Mean that Jesus Descended into Hell?" Catholic News Agency, February 21, 2017. https://www.catholicnewsagency.com/column/53709/what-does-it-mean-that-jesus-descended-into-Hell.

The Navarre Bible: St Matthew's Gospel. New York: Scepter Publishers, 2005.

O'Hearn, Patrick. *Go and Fear Nothing: The Story of Our Lady of Champion*. Huntington, IN: OSV Kids, 2023.

O'Neill, Michael. "Messages of Kibeho." The Miracle Hunter. https://miraclehunter.com/marian_apparitions/messages/kibeho_messages.html

Online Etymology Dictionary, https://www.etymonline.com/.

O'Regan, Mary. "Dónal Enright, a Witness to Many Miracles of Padre Pio, When Padre Pio Lived on This Earth, and Now as St. Pio Intercedes for Us from His Heavenly Home." Mary's Blog, September 24, 2010. https://thepathlesstaken7.blogspot.com/2010/09/donal-enright-witness-to-many-miracles_24.html.

"Our Story." National Shrine of Our Lady of Champion. https://championshrine.org/our-story/.

Pius V, Pope St. *The Catechism of the Council of Trent*. Translated by John A. McHugh, O.P., and Charles J. Callan, O.P. Charlotte, NC: TAN Books, 2017.

Pius X, Pope St. *The Catechism of Pope Saint Pius X*. Gladysdale, Victoria, Australia: Instauratio Press, 1993.

Ruffin, C. Bernard. *Padre Pio: The True Story*. Huntington, IN: Our Sunday Visitor, 2018.

"Second Council of Constantinople." Translated by Henry Percival. From *Nicene and Post-Nicene Fathers*. Second Series. Vol. 14. Edited by Philip Schaff and Henry Wace. Buffalo, NY: Christian Literature Publishing, 1900. Revised and edited for New Advent by Kevin Knight. https://www.newadvent.org/fathers/3812.htm.

Spirago, Francis Rev. *Catechism Explained: Newly Annotated with Corresponding References to the Catechism of the Catholic Church*. Gastonia, NC: TAN Books, 2022.

Staples, Tim. "What Is Hell?" *Catholic Answers*, November 8, 2021. https://www.catholic.com/magazine/online-edition/what-is-Hell.

"Stories of Hell in the Lives of the Saints." Mystics of the Church. www.mysticsofthechurch.com/2013/03/stories-of-Hell-in-lives-of-saints.html.

Teresa of Avila, St. *The Autobiography of St. Teresa of Avila*. Translated by David Lewis. Charlotte, NC: TAN Books, 2012.

Thérèse of Lisieux, St. *The Story of a Soul: The Autobiography of Saint Thérèse of Lisieux*. 3rd ed. Translated by John Clarke, O.C.D. Washington, D.C.: ICS Publications, 1996.

Thigpen, Paul. *A Dictionary of Quotes from the Saints*. Charlotte, NC: TAN Books, 2001.

Vianney, St. John. "The Sewer of Hell." In *Sermons of the Curé of Ars—Excerpts*. Catholic Library Project. https://catholiclibrary.org/library/view?docId=/Tridentine-EN/XCT.086.html&chunk.id=00000037.

About the Authors

DAN BURKE is the founder and president of the Avila Institute for Spiritual Formation, which offers graduate and personal enrichment studies in spiritual theology to priests, deacons, religious, and laity in more than ninety countries and prepares men for seminary in more than one hundred dioceses. Dan is the author or editor of more than fifteen books on authentic Catholic spirituality. To learn more, you can visit SpiritualDirection.com or ApostoliViae.org.

PATRICK O'HEARN is a husband and a father. He holds a master's degree in education from Franciscan University. He has authored or co-authored eight books, including *Parents of the Saints, The Shepherd at the Crib and the Cross, Courtship of the Saints, The Grief of Dads* (co-author), *Go and Fear Nothing, Our Lady of Sorrows,* and *Nursery of Heaven* (co-author). You can visit his website at patrickrohearn.com.

Sophia Institute

Sophia Institute is a nonprofit institution that seeks to nurture the spiritual, moral, and cultural life of souls and to spread the gospel of Christ in conformity with the authentic teachings of the Roman Catholic Church.

Sophia Institute Press fulfills this mission by offering translations, reprints, and new publications that afford readers a rich source of the enduring wisdom of mankind.

Sophia Institute also operates the popular online resource CatholicExchange.com. *Catholic Exchange* provides world news from a Catholic perspective as well as daily devotionals and articles that will help readers to grow in holiness and live a life consistent with the teachings of the Church.

In 2013, Sophia Institute launched Sophia Teachers to renew and rebuild Catholic culture through service to Catholic education. With the goal of nurturing the spiritual, moral, and cultural life of souls, and an abiding respect for the role and work of teachers, we strive to provide materials and programs that are at once enlightening to the mind and ennobling to the heart; faithful and complete, as well as useful and practical.

Sophia Institute gratefully recognizes the Solidarity Association for preserving and encouraging the growth of our apostolate over the course of many years. Without their generous and timely support, this book would not be in your hands.

www.SophiaInstitute.com
www.CatholicExchange.com
www.SophiaTeachers.org